Son
from
Ukraine

A True Story

by
Sandra Upeslacis

FriesenPress

One Printers Way
Altona, MB R0G 0B0
Canada

www.friesenpress.com

ISBN
978-1-03-830320-2 (Hardcover)
978-1-03-830319-6 (Paperback)
978-1-03-830321-9 (eBook)

1. FAMILY & RELATIONSHIPS, ADOPTION & FOSTERING

Distributed to the trade by The Ingram Book Company

Ērikam
For Erik

Table of Contents

December 2000

November 2000
Week One

Kyiv

"Hey, wake up," my husband tells me. "The lady asked you a question."

The flight attendant is smiling. "Can I offer you a beverage, Madame?"

"Uh … yes, please. Water, no ice. Thanks."

My husband, Albert, and I are on the last leg of a long journey from Toronto to Kyiv. We're literally hurtling through the air to an unfamiliar, faraway place.

A child in the row behind us is kicking the back of my husband's seat and telling his mother he's bored and wants to get off the plane. Albert closes his travel book, removes his

glasses and puts them into their case. Shutting his eyes, he pretends not to notice the commotion from behind.

I stare at him for a moment; I'm SO happy we're doing this.

After a time, the child behind us falls quiet. Albert taps my arm. He tells me that despite the fact Ukraine is a huge country with a fascinating history, few visitors' books are available in English. His *Lonely Planet* guide to Russia, Ukraine, and Belarus says it's not a frequent destination for Westerners.

"The country was only recently freed from nearly seventy years of Soviet occupation," he continues. "I bet the Russians made a mess of the place."

The book describes Ukraine as, "a mysterious and exotic country. An ancient centre of Orthodox Christianity and medieval architecture." As my husband reads aloud, I envision strolling along Kyiv's cobblestone streets with our child in a carriage and Albert pointing out historic monuments and structures.

The crow's feet at his temples are becoming more prominent as he half-smiles, turning a page in the book. I love the new look, he's aging gracefully.

Outside the window, clouds veil the view below. According to my wristwatch, we'll be landing in less than an hour.

I haven't lost sight of the fact that the two of us are about to leap into the arms of strangers in a country where we don't speak the language and don't understand the culture.

If there was another way to do this, we might consider it, but the fact remains if you can't have a biological child together, and you really WANT to raise a child together, your best option is an international adoption. Yes, you could become a foster parent or seek an adoption in your own country, but that could take years; these were paths we declined to take.

The two of us are not clueless about parenting. When Albert and I met, he was successfully co-parenting three daughters with his ex-wife. The girls moved back and forth between the two households.

After a whirlwind romance, we married in less than a year and I became an instant stepmom to his lovely girls.

The beginning months (and years) were a bit rocky. I was the "new arrival" who struggled to fit in to the established rhythm of an existing, well-functioning family. I had to fall into line to keep the peace, and hope that somebody noticed.

Back to my original point, Albert and I want to raise a child together—his fourth, my first. Hence the flight to Kyiv, where we are about to meet some people who are adept at wrestling Ukrainian government bureaucracy to the ground.

These people were corralled for us by Laryssa Hrehoriv, a petite adoption agent living in suburban Toronto whose expertise is Ukraine. Within minutes of meeting the woman in the doorway of her home, I knew she had the intellectual and emotional weight to give us the straight goods. Laryssa provided a frank but hopeful description of international adoption requirements, and stared us down while asking if we had the fortitude to actually see it through.

"Yes, of course," we answered. We were impressed by Laryssa's approach, and hired her to assist.

A social worker did a home study mandated by the Province of Ontario. We assembled the material requested by Canada and Ukraine, from financial statements to health and career information, and photos and information about our home, family, and community (in other words, we voluntarily underwent a full body cavity search).

We were fingerprinted by the Royal Canadian Mounted Police and cleared by Interpol, and then we gathered letters from close friends, family and the reverend of our church attesting to our good character and suitability to raise an adopted child.

We're now cleared to become parents of a child from Ukraine.

The plan is to return to Canada within four to six weeks with a new sibling for the girls and the newest member of our large extended family.

For several months leading up to the trip, I studied Ukrainian language audiotapes so that in a pinch, we might somehow be able to communicate with local people. But we won't be on our own all that much. Laryssa arranged for a local translator, facilitator, and driver to accompany us during our stay.

I pull a soft three-ring binder out from my carry-on bag and scan the first section, which has contact information for people we have meetings with in Kyiv. Flipping the page, I read the "key phrases in Ukrainian" sheet and repeat them to myself, several times.

"*Pryvit*. Hello."

"*Dyakuyu*. Thank you."

"*Tak*. Yes."

"*Ni*. No."

"*Dobryy vechir*. Good evening."

"*Rada vas bachyty*. Nice to see you."

"*Do pobachennya*. Goodbye."

I move to the section in the folder with emails from Laryssa. I've drawn a star beside a series of adoption support posts she has shared from the Adoption from Ukraine Internet Club, about raising a child who has spent time in a post-Soviet children's home. The posts are eye-opening, to say the least.

One in particular, "The Long-term Effects of Institutionalization on Children from Eastern Europe and the Former Soviet Union," describes some of the ways children in this environment might express themselves and behave due to their life circumstances, that Albert and I would be unfamiliar with. It also points to ways of helping these children thrive in their new family.

Prepared by the Parent Network for The Post-Institutionalized Child, possible emotional and psychological manifestations among the children could include aggressive, passive or autistic-like behaviour, and issues with attachment and bonding. Developmental delays and learning disabilities, language and cognitive disorders, are also discussed, along with potential medical problems, including fetal alcohol syndrome.

Are we ready for this?

I don't dispute the findings of researchers who know what they're talking about, but despite the potential challenges, I'm not discouraged. There's a child in Ukraine destined for our family, I'm sure of it. Love will conquer all. We'll find a way.

I reread what I previously scribbled at the bottom of the first page of posts: "Love. Support. Family." That's what I want to give our son or daughter from Ukraine.

Underlined in red marker is a paragraph in another email to me from Laryssa that I need to remind myself of: "I would like to impress on you that being outspoken and extremely demanding in Ukraine will only set up potential road blocks for your adoption process and would also jeopardize the families traveling behind you. This is the nature and mentality of Ukrainians. They are proud people who view Westerners as often having the advantage of privilege. A humble but firm attitude is the best approach."

Hmmm. I will try to hold my tongue in Ukraine. Scorched earth tactics obviously won't go over well.

In the next section of the folder, there's a newspaper clipping from the *Kyiv Post*, called, "Foreign Adoptions on the Rise." It notes that adoptions of Ukrainian children by foreigners have skyrocketed since the government ban on the process was lifted in 1996, even almost doubling between 1998 and 1999.

The first foreign couple legally allowed to adopt a child from Ukraine under the new 1996 regulations was Canadian, of Ukrainian ancestry. Seems like a good omen!

Albert and I have an instinctive affinity for Ukraine. Citizens of any country doomed to live under the Soviet boot experienced decades of trauma and human rights violations, among other horrors.

My family, and my husband's, lost their homes, livelihoods, and loved ones in Latvia during World War Two. They were forced to leave the land their families had farmed for hundreds of years while the armies of Nazi Germany and Soviet Russia fought over the tiny Baltic country, burning and destroying everything in the process.

Our families crossed an ocean as war refugees, had to build new lives from nothing, and could not visit their homeland or reunite with family members who remained behind until decades later. There is common grief and grit among ethnic Latvians and Ukrainians.

Before Ukraine was forced to join Russia's Soviet Union in 1922, there were hundreds of years of chaotic history between the two nations. But the mass executions and *Holodomor*—"death by hunger"—that Soviet leader Joseph Stalin inflicted on Ukrainians in the 1930s was particularly coldblooded, killing 10 million people. Then World War Two came, bringing more devastation, with Ukraine ultimately remaining captive … you get the picture.

Among the Latvians who sought to escape the horrors of World War Two were nearly 15,000 who immigrated to Canada. The trauma of losing their homeland never went away. Latvian Canadians were hell-bent on maintaining their cultural identity and passing it on to their children so that the dream of regaining a free Latvia could live on. In 2016, Canada Census reported more than 30,000 people of Latvian origin living in the country.

As a child attending Latvian language "Saturday school" in Toronto, I was made to watch a movie about The Corner House, a building in the Latvian capital of Riga. The House was occupied by the invading Russian army/KGB in 1940–1941, and Latvian citizens were interrogated and jailed there.

The remains of young Latvian men who'd been tortured and murdered by the Russians offered brutal visual evidence in the movie of what went on. I never forgot what I saw, which I now understand was the point of the exercise. And while it was only one example of what happened under Russian occupation, I'm tormented to this day. (The Corner House eventually became the KGB's Latvia headquarters, where decades of interrogation and human rights abuses by the Russians are now being unearthed, but that's another story.)

An announcement over the plane's intercom brings me out of my reflections.

"Ladies and gentlemen, we will be landing in Kyiv shortly. We will collect any remaining items to discard momentarily. Please, put your seat in the upright position and fasten your seat belt."

******

A well-dressed gentleman in a black wool coat and hat is holding a sign with my husband's name on it in the baggage area of Kyiv's Boryspil International Airport. We walk purposefully toward him; the man nods respectfully.

"*Hallo*. I am Boris. Welcome to Kyiv."

Albert and the driver exchange quick handshakes.

"Thank you for giving us a lift," my husband says.

"You are most welcome," Boris retorts. "Please, come this way."

The driver points to my suitcase with his gloved hand, takes the handle, and rolls it toward the main exit doors. Albert follows him, pulling his own suitcase. I trail behind.

We make our way to an outdoor parking lot and stop at a black German sedan with tinted windows. Boris puts our luggage into the trunk and opens the front passenger door. A blonde woman with a purple paisley scarf draping her navy coat steps out. She introduces herself as Sofia, our Ukrainian adoption facilitator. Her handshake is firm. I remember the lady's name from the contacts list in my binder.

"I hope you had an enjoyable flight. I'm very pleased to meet you, Albert and Sandra, and to support you in Ukraine."

"Nice to meet you too, Sofia," my husband responds.

"I have spoken to Laryssa about you. I studied your file and have a good sense of the task at hand. My team and I will do our very best to help you find your child. You will bring home a wonderful boy or girl from Ukraine. We will make this journey together."

"*Dyakuyu.* Thank you," I say, my eyes tearing up.

Sofia's eyes widen. "Ah, you speak Ukrainian?"

"No, but I've tried to learn a few words and phrases to show respect for your country."

"Wonderful. Thank you. Please, Albert and Sandra, get in the car. Boris will take you to the hotel. I will leave now and meet you for dinner later. Boris will give you the address of the restaurant. It is on the same street as your hotel, just a few blocks away. You can easily walk there. I suppose you would like to rest for a few hours before we discuss the arrangements for the coming days and weeks? Goodbye for now."

"Bye." Albert's voice is hoarse from the flight.

I drop into the comfortable leather seat in the rear of the car. My husband, beside me, leans far back against the headrest. He squeezes my hand and closes his eyes. I shut mine, too. When I open them a few moments later we're on a highway, headed for the city.

Soon, we exit off a downward ramp onto a wide urban street. There's a sudden sputtering sound, and then, a loud thud. The car stalls. Thankfully, Boris is able to glide the vehicle to the shoulder.

The driver tries to restart the car several times, but fails. He turns around in his seat.

"*Hallo*, we have slight problem."

"Obviously," I whisper to my husband.

Albert opens his eyes and sits straight up, paying close attention. I watch Boris remove his gloves and lift his small hands, moving his fingers and wrists in a rotating fashion while speaking quickly in Russian or Ukrainian, I have no idea which language. I can make out the sound of the word "*mashina,*" which sounds like a word for "car" in Latvian, but nothing else.

The chauffeur looks at Albert; my husband stares blankly back, as he can't comprehend the message.

Boris puts his hat down on the front seat.

"Please, one moment. I will fix. Do not be concerned."

Boris gets out of the car. He lifts the front hood and then retrieves some tools from the trunk.

"Do you want to get out and help him?" I ask.

"Are you kidding?"

"Uh … no."

"Leave the man to his work. I'm no mechanic."

"Okay."

I close my eyes again and try to sleep. The car quickly becomes chilly. I open my eyes and look outside. The hood of the car remains raised. The ground is frozen white. Large ice-covered trees line the broad roadway. The temperature must be below freezing. A row of tall, Soviet-era apartment complexes is set back from the road. Across the other side of the street are more apartment buildings.

I place my arm under my husband's and wriggle in close against his shoulder. We hold each other to try and stay warm. After a while, Albert gets out of the car. I hear the two men talking, and then my husband returns to the backseat.

"Well?"

"Well, nothing. I have no idea what's wrong. I'm sure Boris will take care of it, or maybe he's called someone about it."

"Just our luck."

"Yeah."

We hear the driver move tools around under the hood, bang things, watch him return inside, make a phone call, go back outside, and come inside again to try and start the engine. Eventually, it works.

Not long after, we arrive at a multistorey modern hotel in suburban Kyiv called the Luba. Boris mounts the stone stairs to the main entrance together with us, helping with our luggage. At the top of the staircase, he hands Albert a piece of paper with an address for a restaurant and the time of 20:00 written.

"For you; enjoy your dinner. Until tomorrow," the chauffeur says.

Albert thanks and tips him, then watches as Boris descends the staircase.

We enter the Luba through an arched glass walkway and head to the reception desk.

"Good afternoon," the woman working the desk greets us. "Yes, I see the reservation. May I ask the purpose of your visit?"

The skinny young clerk is verifying our passports for check-in. She has a doe-like, translucent-white face and a tiny nose. I assume her real job is being a top fashion model and the hotel is just temporary work, but then I see that all of the other female workers behind the mahogany counter are rail-thin and beautiful and could pose for *Vogue* magazine.

The clerk's question seems odd. Why would she care what my husband and I are doing in Ukraine?

I'm eager to get to the guest room and lie down. But the woman persists. She raises her eyebrows and pushes her pointy chin upward in anticipation of an explanation.

Albert takes a step back, deferring to me to respond.

"We're here on personal business," I explain.

"What is nature of personal *beezness*?" The broken English is charming.

My husband and I exchange quizzical looks. I can tell he won't speak, so I take the lead again. "We've come to Ukraine to adopt a child."

"Ah, yes. Canadians! You have visitation here. We have experience of other family at our hotel. Please, enjoy your stay."

The clerk writes some notes on an official-looking document. She turns to my spouse and presents him with the room key, despite the fact that I am standing directly in front of her and she has to lean past me to reach his hand. The fashion model also hands him a pen to sign for the room.

"How are you paying, sir? Cash? Credit card? You must pay three days' advance; 400 *hryvnias*, please." The woman won't look at me.

I hand her American cash. She takes it and calculates the currency conversion. Without turning her head towards me, the clerk counts out change in *hryvnias* for the cost of the room, hands it to my husband, writes something on a small piece of paper, and gives it to him. Albert pretends to read the receipt, which is in Cyrillic script, and puts the money into his pocket.

"Thank you," he says.

I scan the lobby. It has an airy, minimalist feel, with white marble floors, muted floral wallpaper, and a lofty white ceiling. The space is devoid of couches or chairs, but flourishing plants are strategically placed throughout. Abstract oil paintings dot the walls with splashes of vibrant colour.

There's a glass-walled bar inside the hotel's main entrance, off to one side. Men in dark suits are downing drinks and watching sports matches on a small screen TV. A handful of women in revealing dresses and spiked heels closely attend to the men. Their pronounced makeup exaggerates the effect of the sexy chitchat.

Soldiers in fatigues with machine guns guard the hotel entrance; others patrol the foyer. They are an indication that the country is in transition after the breakup of the Soviet Union. What direction will Ukraine ultimately take? The country's president, Leonid Kuchma, is considered by many in the West to be a puppet of Russian president, Vladimir Putin. In Ukraine's recent national election, there were allegations that Kuchma's re-election was not necessarily clean, that voting irregularities were seen. The nation's ties to its former oppressor apparently remain strong.

"Okay, let's go," Albert says, taking my arm.

The doors of the mirrored elevator off the lobby open slowly. Albert presses twelve on the silver keypad. The ride up is slightly bumpy but swift. As the doors reopen, an elderly female concierge greets us, bowing her head.

"*Pasport*," the lady requests as we step out to the twelfth-floor landing.

I unzip my carry-on bag, retrieve our passports, and hand them over. The woman reviews the documents, writes something in a ledger on a table behind her, and returns them to me.

She motions for my husband to show her our room key and receipt. He provides them. The lady notes the room number, and then presents another, smaller key.

"*Dyakuyu*. Thank you," I tell her.

The concierge says a few words back to me, but I shrug to let her know I don't understand what she's trying to convey. Tipping her head to one side, the old woman falls silent.

Away from the landing, we head left down a cavernous hallway toward our guest room. The corridor is dim, but I can make out blue velvet wallpaper and brown wainscotting along the way. Our luggage wheels reverberate loudly along the wooden floor.

The two keys open one set of doors each, leading us to the guest room. Inside the sizeable space are two twin beds with a night table and lamp positioned between them. In the middle of the room, French windows are framed with heavy teal drapes.

My husband moves our suitcases near the wardrobe beside the bathroom. I flick on the switch in the bathroom and wait a bit, but the light doesn't work at all. At least the toilet and stall look clean. Fresh white towels adorn the rack beside the bathing area. There's no shower curtain, but the water in the sink works, so I believe we'll be fine.

"I'm beat, but I don't think I can sleep," Albert says.

The wing-backed chair by the window embraces him comfortably as he returns to reading his *Lonely Planet* guide. The late afternoon sun streams into the room, spilling light onto his book. The navy turtleneck sweater he's wearing handsomely outlines his face and perfectly complements his gray-brown hair. This is my man's happy place: anywhere he can read a good book.

I unpack our clothes, put them in the wardrobe, and lie down on the bed nearest the window. The room is a bit cold, so I grab the throw blanket at the foot of the bed and soon fall asleep.

A while later, I feel my husband moving my shoulder to wake me.

"Hey, we need to get ready to go out for dinner."

The sky outside the window is now dark and clear. Lights twinkle below, illuminating the wide city street, dusted from snowfall.

Albert jokes our guest room could have electronic bugging devices left over from Soviet times. He conducts a mock sweep, lifting and inspecting the night lamp and table. Mattresses are turned over, the headboard checked, and the antique receiver of the phone drilled into the wall is unscrewed to verify everything is clear.

I tease him that Ukrainian secret service people are in the next room, listening with electronic devices to our Latvian-Canadian banter, frustrated they can't understand what we're saying.

"Those who worship Vladimir Putin should move to Russia and never come back!" I loudly declare.

"They'll be coming to arrest you any moment now," Albert jokes. "Let's make the two beds into one, so we can sleep close together like we always do."

We lift the night table and place it beside the wing-backed chair, push the beds together, and change into warmer clothes for our evening out.

"I wish we had a mobile phone on the trip," I complain. "It's weird that we can't call or text our family to let them know we arrived well in Kyiv."

"Remember what we decided? The overseas mobile charges our Canadian provider was proposing for five or six weeks in Ukraine could quickly add up to a thousand dollars or more, based on all the people we want to stay in touch with. If you recall, I made a group email for my whole family and yours. I'm sure we'll come across an internet cafe soon and we can send emails home whenever we want. Easy peasy."

"Oh, right. I forgot."

"And, we can always use the landline in our hotel room should there be an emergency. So, let's get moving now or we'll be late."

Mamma's Kitchen

"Mamma's Kitchen" resto-bar is a welcome twenty-minute walk from our hotel in the brisk evening air.

Inside, Sofia waves us over to a table in the heart of the eatery. A young woman is seated beside her.

"Good evening! Glad you found the restaurant," Sofia cheerily declares.

"Hello," I reply. "Yes, this place is as you said, just up the street from our hotel. It's nice."

"Would you like something to drink? I will order it for you", Sofia asks as we sit.

"Local beer would be great," Albert responds, smiling.

"Water for me," I add. "Non-carbonated. Thank you."

The crowded venue is quaint and inviting with kitschy decor, crammed-in dining tables, and charming lace curtains covering vaulted windows.

A waitress hoists hefty dinner portions on her arms as she strides past our table. I catch a whiff of cabbage, garlic, and pork and suddenly become hungry. The aroma reminds me of my mom's cabbage soup. While most tables are packed with patrons enjoying a meal out, a few couples are on the dance floor by the bar, keeping step with European pop music playing on a nearby television screen.

Above the booming conversations of other patrons, Sofia introduces her dining companion, Iryna, our translator.

Iryna stands to greet us. She is tall and lanky with dark, short-cropped hair. Bright red lipstick accentuates her gaunt face.

"Hello. Wonderful to meet you," she says animatedly. Her voice is a bit low, as though fighting a cold. She confidently extends her arm; the handshake is clammy.

Iryna sits back down. Her words are delivered methodically, in near-perfect English as she recounts her experience and education, confirming to us her ability to translate the various documents we'll need to address during our stay. Her tone is somber and direct, but there's genuine compassion in her voice. In between sentences, she takes an occasional sip of tea; her silver bracelets jangle when she lifts her arm to her mouth. I presume she's in her early to mid-twenties because she tells us she recently married and completed her university education.

Sofia carefully observes our reactions. She's rounder, shorter, and older than Iryna and has a caring, motherly face. She jots down notes in a leather-bound notebook while Iryna speaks. The paisley scarf is now wrapped over a mauve sweater dress.

Back in Canada, Laryssa, our adoption agent, shared that apart from helping people adopt children, Sofia also heads the Ukrainian arm of a Canadian-based charitable organization that supports children's homes and other humanitarian efforts. The nonprofit has provided millions of dollars in aid to Ukraine since its inception in 1993. Our well-connected facilitator will be advantageous to us, I'm sure of it.

I'm listening to the points our dining companions are making about what we'll need to do together as we make our way through the Ukrainian adoption system.

"As you know, I've read your file," Sofia remarks, "and we will soon clarify how we will work together to achieve a positive result. But first, I would like to hear directly from you, Albert and Sandra, in your own words, as to why you made the decision to adopt a child from Ukraine?"

While Albert recounts our story, my mind travels back to the day we decided to adopt. Simply put, we wanted to feel good about our new life together. If we couldn't achieve a pregnancy through the latest technological methods available in Canada, we'd have to change course.

We sat in on sessions run by the Adoption Council of Ontario about ways to adopt children in Canada and abroad. We learned we're drawn to vulnerable children in other parts of the world, where providing a child with basic necessities can be a monumental struggle for the people who live there.

A council speaker clarified that a child is not always living in a "children's home" because their parents have died. Economic, social, and political pressures can force people to relinquish their children because they do not have the means to look after them.

We considered and researched options for adopting a boy or girl from Latvia, Romania, Russia and Ukraine.

Latvia fell away as a consideration when we learned the country was in the midst of rewriting her adoption laws and our efforts could potentially be stalled. We lost interest in adopting from Romania and Russia because the countries demanded pre-selection of a child before even meeting them or visiting the country.

We ultimately landed on Ukraine for two reasons. The first was a personal connection. My maternal grandmother lived for a time in Kharkiv. During World War One, when the German and Russian armies were fighting over territory in Latvia, the destruction caused by both armies plundering the countryside left inhabitants no choice but to seek safer territory elsewhere.

Thousands left their Latvian homeland, mostly to places in the Russian empire. My grandmother's family was able to find work in Kharkiv, where she gave birth to two sons, both of whom died as infants and are buried there. After the war, my grandmother and her family returned to her native Latvia, where she raised four children. Together with her children, Grandma left Latvia as a war refugee during World War Two, eventually moving to the United States and, finally, Canada.

Every few years since my grandmother's death I'm reminded of her when cleaning out drawers or closets in my home. Several pairs of her hand-knit slippers are inevitably kicking around. My grandma always gifted her homemade creations to family members, providing so many pairs in varying colours and patterns that there was a running joke among the grandchildren about her "slipper factory."

The slippers seemed insignificant at the time, but they're now a cherished link to my grandmother and signal the continuity of family through generations.

The second and principal reason we chose Ukraine, however, was because the country has a well-organized, highly professional and humane approach to international adoption.

"Once we decided on Ukraine," I hear Albert saying as I rejoin the conversation, "we never looked back. Many kind people lent a hand along the way."

"Well, thank you for expressing your intentions, they are very useful for Iryna and I in executing our work," Sofia explains. She raises her index finger. "We will take one step at a time. We do not control the timeline. We engage with the required government, institutional, and legal authorities according to their availability to complete the adoption process."

Iryna interjects, "But of course, we will seek to complete the work within a reasonable time and within the budget that was provided by Laryssa's agency in Canada."

"That sounds good," Albert says.

Our beverages arrive with a thump on the table. The beer is served in a tall, chunky glass rimmed with gold. The elegant water bottle has a blue label with feminine lettering. My husband lifts his hefty mug, and clanks it against my water glass.

"Cheers," he says, taking a sip.

"To all of us," I add. I'm so parched I down half of the glass in one go.

Iryna announces that Sofia has arranged an appointment for us with Lyudmyla Kravchenko, director of Ukraine's National Adoption Centre at the Ministry of Education and Science. The appointment is for 10:00 tomorrow; we'll need to be outside the hotel by 9:30 sharp. Based on the portfolio of information we provided, the director will likely propose a specific boy or girl for us to visit, provided we accept her recommendation.

Sofia nods her agreement and smiles emphatically to underscore she's pleased with the appointment that has been confirmed on our behalf.

I'm fixed on the statement Iryna's made about tomorrow's meeting, how we might learn about the file of a boy or girl we may be invited to consider. What excellent news! Albert and I just landed in Kyiv and already we're on the cusp of meeting a child who could possibly become the newest member of our family.

But will it really be *that* easy? A meeting with adoption officials one day after we arrive and then we're off to meet the child?

Iryna describes the menu for "Mamma's Kitchen." Albert and I opt for meatball soup; the ladies both order *vareniki*—potato dumplings. The local beer accompanies our meal.

I am seated facing the dance floor. A middle-aged man in tight leather pants is rotating his hips to the beat of the music. His belly hangs low over his belt, and his eyes are glued to a much younger dance partner. I wonder what the teenage girl is thinking about the man, with his slicked-back hair and broken front tooth protruding when he smiles. Do the chains around his neck and half-open shirt entice or repel? I can't tell; the girl's face shows no emotion.

After we eat, the translator straightens the red cape on her shoulders and describes the procedure for the following day's visit to the National Adoption Centre at the Ministry of Education and Science.

"Please wear business-appropriate attire and be ready to address any questions in your adoption portfolio," she exclaims. "We have your complete documentation, which has been translated into Ukrainian and notarized. Sofia and I have both reviewed it and are well aware of your situation."

Sofia adds, "We understand that you wish to adopt a boy or girl, preferably under age two, but this is not a mandatory element."

"Yes," Albert responds, nodding. "We've spent a lot of time preparing the portfolio, so I could likely recite most of the information in my sleep."

"Very good." Iryna's dark eyes twitch as she speaks.

I'm impressed with the duo's approach, and Albert lets the ladies know we'll be ready to go at half past nine the next morning, as agreed. My husband puts his beer glass down on the orange-and-white checkered tablecloth with a clunk.

My eyes return to the leather-clad man and his date. He is laser focused on the teenager swaying her hips in a slinky blue dress and determined to fulfil his agenda. He's trying to master the twist, slowly bending his knees, moving his buttocks ever closer to the floor with each thump of the music, raising his elbows and turning his torso from side to side, sweat dripping down his face. I catch my husband smirking at the duo, as well. It's clear we're both wondering whether the man will fall or manage to twist all the way down. Luckily, the fellow makes it all the way to the floor. He grunts loudly at the end, punctuating the dance move with his audible exclamation point. The girl finally cracks a smile.

The dinner bill arrives. Albert counts out a stack of *hryvnias* and drops them onto a small metal tray on our table. Sofia looks up beyond her round eyeglasses. She stops writing the notes she's been taking in her leather book, signaling the evening's business has concluded. I watch her place the pen and notebook into a large brown handbag, stand up, and sling the bag over her shoulder.

"Well, we will walk you back to your hotel." Sofia smiles broadly and touches my back. "Tomorrow, the work begins."

After the long trip and dinner out, I'm craving sleep.

My husband and I ride the elevator back up to the twelfth floor of the Luba hotel. The doors open; a male concierge stands guard at the elevator landing. Albert presents our room keys and points to the ledger. The man asks for his passport and mine, which we provide. He finally waves us through.

"What's with all the security checks?" I ask.

"Where do you think you are, Canada, where you can just walk in anywhere and nobody cares who you are or what you're doing?" Albert responds. "Things are different here."

We make our way back to the guest room.

Crushed with exhaustion, I wash up in the dark bathroom and lie down on the bed. I'm on my side, facing my husband. He starts snoring before I can say goodnight. I roll onto my back, stare up at the crystal chandelier hanging from the ceiling, and quickly fall asleep.

I am awakened in the middle of the night by a woman's ear-splitting scream. I sit up in bed and tap my husband's side to rouse him. At first it sounds like the noise is coming from the hallway, but then I realize it's from the guest room next door. Furniture is being thrown and a man is yelling.

"Did you hear that?" I whisper.

"Yeah. Forget it. It's nothing, just people coming back from a party. Go back to sleep." Albert turns over on his side, away from me.

Frozen with fear, I lay back down and nuzzle in close against my husband's back, pulling the bed covers over my head.

The man and woman seem to be arguing. Something glass is smashed. A heavy object is thrown against the wall. The woman shrieks again. The man speaks rapidly; he seems to be ordering the woman around. It's quiet for a moment, then I hear the bedpost being pounded hard against the wall, again and again. The lovemaking is aggressive. The woman groans loudly and the man keeps shouting. There are slapping noises.

After several minutes, the thumping stops. I hear the man's voice for a short time afterward. Then everything falls silent.

I wonder if the woman is a sex worker, if she's been raped, or whether they are a couple that enjoys rough sex. I can't fall back asleep. I worry that the woman may have been murdered, but I'm too scared to do anything about it.

The reality of being in Ukraine, and not in Canada, is setting in.

Hoping and Waiting

As we leave our guest room to head downstairs in search of a restaurant for breakfast, I ask my husband if we should tell any hotel staff what we heard the night before.

"Absolutely not," he snorts. "It's none of our business."

I inspect the rug and door from the neighboring guest room for signs of blood. There aren't any. We stride down the hallway.

The mature concierge from the previous day is again on the job by the elevator. She checks our room keys against the ledger on the desk beside her but doesn't ask for our passports. The lady nods that we can take the elevator down.

I have trouble understanding what is going on. If someone takes an elevator up, provides their passport and has a room key and payment receipt, it means they're legitimate guests. The next morning, if they're still in possession of room keys and wish to go down, then they obviously continue to be paying guests.

"For some reason, the Luba staff think there are people with nefarious intentions working the building, posing as guests," I comment to Albert.

"I told you last night, this isn't Canada. It's Ukraine. The country has only been free of Russia for nine years. The guys in military uniforms with machine guns downstairs are not window dressing. We have nothing to worry about, but there's a reason why things are how they are."

"And what do you think that is?"

"I don't know, to keep order? Keep people in line?"

The Luba hotel's ground floor restaurant is near the mirrored elevators by the lobby. It's a large, sunken-level open space with floor-to-ceiling windows. Tables for two and four are set with formal white tablecloths and polished silverware. A single red rose in a crystal vase graces every table. The wooden dining chairs have comfortable dark velvet cushions.

Two bored-looking soldiers in fatigues pace the dining room, guns at their sides.

The tables have no menus. Customers sit and wait, and eventually a server arrives carrying a silver platter. He carefully presents each guest with a plate containing a small wedge of cheese, thin slice of ham, and dark rye bread. A tiny espresso coffee and a small glass of juice round out the meal. Water? No.

I quickly learn, there is no such thing as a second cup of coffee at breakfast. The formally attired wait staff are courteous and have passable English, but they become cross when a guest requests anything beyond what is brought as the standard meal.

The place seats about a hundred guests, but we are among only a dozen or so up and about for the early meal.

After breakfast, Albert and I exit the hotel and walk in the same direction we'd gone the previous evening to get to Mamma's Kitchen. We'd passed a shopping complex with a graphic sign designating an internet cafe and wanted to head there to send emails home to let family and friends know we've arrived and are well looked after.

I ask a woman behind the perfume counter in the shopping centre for directions to the internet cafe similar to the way I've heard Russian speakers use during previous visits to Latvia. I enunciate the "e" in cafe as a short "*eh*" instead of "*ay*." It works. The woman points to a nearby escalator leading up to the second floor of the building.

"*Dyakuyu*. Thank you," I say, but she ignores me.

The internet cafe is dark, with several rows of desks and computers, the majority being occupied by adolescent boys playing video games or watching internet pornography. The only computer available is in a back corner and it's covered in sticky filth. I refuse to touch the keyboard or sit on the hard plastic chair. Albert types the email. I ask him to hurry, as the airless room reeks of nicotine and semen. I make a mental note to put the disposable hand wipes I brought with me from Canada into our backpack for future outings.

Outside the Luba hotel at precisely 9:30, Iryna steps out of Boris' black sedan. She tells us the chauffeur wants us to know his car is now in excellent working condition with no further repairs needed. Albert gives Boris a smile and a thumbs up; the driver tips his hat in response.

Getting into the vehicle, Iryna notes Sofia will join us at the National Adoption Centre at the Ministry of Education and Science.

Boris maneuvers the streets of Kyiv past imposing Orthodox churches, Baroque structures, and stone monuments like a rally driver, passing long lines of cars and ignoring traffic signals or signs. There are no pavement markings to separate the roadway lanes, so cars drive all the way up to the curb. Orthodox Christian icons hanging in Boris' front windshield bob up and down as we swish across three lanes of a major thoroughfare. The chauffeur evidently wants to ensure our prompt arrival at the ministry.

Access to the imposing stone building is off a back parking lot. Our driver presents some papers to a military officer at the lot entrance. The man writes some information on a clipboard and allows us to pass through.

The enormous green wood door creaks as we step over the threshold into a dark landing. Iryna flicks on a light switch and we jog three flights up the stone stairs to the appropriate floor. The light dies as we reach the third-floor landing.

Along a gloomy corridor that seems to stretch on forever, hundreds of people stand in line. This is where people from all over the world seeking to adopt a child from Ukraine have come. While it places us at the very back of the queue, I'm impressed that so many couples and individuals from faraway places have arrived with the same purpose in mind. On the downside, it also means there could be a long wait for our appointment with the director, Mrs. Kravchenko.

Sofia has been standing in for us. As we move into the line, she steps out and tells us to stay in place. Albert and I wait while the Ukrainian consultants head to the front of the hallway to see what's going on. I can hear fragments of conversations in front of us in Italian, French, and English.

I wonder how long the wait will be. After about thirty minutes of standing in place in high-heeled boots, my toes are feeling pinched. I move from side to side, changing position.

Albert suggests I be patient; we're in no hurry to go anywhere. We've come a very long way to find our child. We can wait.

I look into my husband's eyes. They're red, still weary from the long voyage. They remind me of my own punishing fatigue. I'm struggling with the time change and the lack of sleep after the late-night ruckus in the room next to ours. To top things off, the building is apparently not heated. Despite all the people in the hallway offering collective body heat, the enormous edifice is cold. I wish I'd worn my thermal leggings under my woolen skirt. I jump up and down on the spot to warm up.

I count and conclude that every fourth light along the hallway is working. The near-darkness is starting to feel oppressive, and the dank, chilly air is getting tiresome. I wonder if the lights are turned off to save energy or if the government can't afford to replace the bulbs?

Four hours later, and approximately ten metres closer to the National Adoption Centre door, we remain standing. My husband and I try to laugh away our shared frustration.

"Things could be worse," Albert says. "We could be told to wait outside the building, where it's even colder."

Miraculously, having re-verified our appointment, Iryna and Sofia soon return and ask us to follow them. Mrs. Kravchenko is waiting for us in her office.

My spirits lift. We all hurry down the hall. We are shown to a cramped room with long narrow tables and stiff wooden chairs. A half dozen other couples are already waiting in the room, ostensibly readying for their own chance to meet Mrs. Kravchenko.

We all take a seat. It's pleasantly warm in the space. I can finally remove my coat and stretch my legs under the table. I rotate my ankles to invigorate my feet. Albert looks up at a book shelf on the wall. I glance over to it, as well; the titles on the book spines are all in Cyrillic.

A door swings open in the centre of the room, and a middle-aged woman in a tailored suit walks out. She has a commanding presence. I instantly know who she is. The gait is steady, though slow, and with each step taken the lady rocks slightly to one side. She calls out, "Upeslacis, Albert," and my husband quickly stands up. The woman motions for us to step into the inner office. Iryna follows us in. Sofia remains in the waiting room, texting on her mobile.

The sunny room is comfortably furnished, with two large bookshelves and plush brocade armchairs. Framed photos of babies and toddlers cover the walls.

Mrs. Kravchenko sits carefully down behind her sizeable oak desk. She takes a deep breath, and crosses her hands together, elbows leaning on the desk. Her head turns slowly from side to side, eyes moving between my husband's gaze and mine. She is sizing us up. I count ten steamboats, then screw up the courage to speak.

"*Dyakuyu*. Thank you."

I repeat the words and burst into tears, but I quickly compose myself. I can sense Mrs. Kravchenko's generosity of spirit.

Lyudmyla Kravchenko does not speak English, and the meeting is brief. Iryna translates the few technical points the director is making about international adoption agreements between Ukraine and Canada, but the information is general and does not specifically address our case.

Mrs. Kravchenko references the new adoption laws in Ukraine, which have added an extra restriction for foreign couples. We are only allowed to adopt a child who has been on the National Adoption Centre's list for a year or more. My husband and I nod our heads, expressing our agreement and understanding.

We try to convey our gratitude for the meeting, using hand signals and a few more words I remember in Ukrainian.

"*Rada vas pobachyty*," I try to say. "Nice to see you."

The corners of Mrs. Kravchenko's mouth turn upward. Her face remains serious, but I can tell the effort to speak her native language is appreciated. She stands up, spontaneously hugs me, and shakes my husband's hand. The meeting is over.

"*Dopobachennya*. Goodbye," I exclaim as we are ordered back into the room with the other couples and the long tables.

Sofia encourages us to stay seated and remain calm while she leaves the room with Iryna to attend to other business. I can't bring myself down to the level of calm. I'm too excited!

I envision myself standing on the edge of a diving board. All I have to do is take one step further, jump up, and I'll be off, swooping down and splashing into the water below. But the wait is long and grueling. We've now been at the government building for hours. Albert puts his arm around my waist, telling me he believes we'll soon have some news.

In less than an hour, our Ukrainian consultants waltz triumphantly back into the room to let us know we'll be returning to the National Adoption Centre the very next day for the formal meeting with Mrs. Kravchenko. The first encounter was apparently just a "meet and greet."

On the drive back to the hotel, the streets of Kyiv are a blur. It's now snowing hard. Boris is no longer hurrying to get us anywhere on time. He observes the traffic signals and quietly smokes a cigarette. Iryna is in the front seat beside him, scribbling on a long writing pad. I feel my husband's fingers interlace tightly with those of my right hand. We sit silently in the back seat, our bodies falling closely in against one another, holding each other up with the little energy we have left.

******

On our second visit to the National Adoption Centre at the Ministry of Education and Science, I anticipate another long, slow-moving queue in the dark hallway with its yellow-brown walls. But the line is moving faster than the previous day, and we are only made to wait our turn for about an hour and a half.

I've brought along a bottle of water and granola bars for Albert and I to share. It shocks me that people in Ukraine seem to go for hours without eating, drinking, or using the toilet. Iryna is surprised when I ask her where the building's cafeteria is located and if it would be possible to get some takeout coffee.

"Sorry, no, it is not possible. There is no cafeteria here and no coffee to take away."

It occurs to me our translator might be appalled by my request for coffee in the middle of such serious business, but the reality is people need their caffeine! I'm thinking the Government of Ukraine could earn some income from a small takeout shop in the building where a portion of the proceeds could be used to replace the missing hallway lightbulbs and also possibly heat the building. Given the several hundred people standing in our line alone who are flush with Western cash, the profits could be worthwhile.

"A coffee and donut place could make a killing here," I tell my husband, who smiles wryly before burying his head back in his book.

Things begin to look up when Sofia pops her head out from a door near the front end of the hallway. She calls out to Iryna and gestures for all of us to go to her. Albert and I sprint to the open door and go inside. After a short wait in a closet-sized space with room for one chair only, we are brought once again to the anteroom with the long tables together with other couples who have been summoned to see Mrs. Kravchenko.

I feel optimistic, and whisper to Albert, "This must be it!"

He smiles elatedly back at me, squeezing my hand.

Through the wall, in another adjacent room, I hear our facilitator raising her voice, engaged in lively conversation. Other women's voices are interspersed with hers. Drawers are opened and slammed shut, and someone repeatedly says, "*Ni*. No." Every once in a while, I believe I can hear Sofia saying, "*Tak*. Yes."

About two hours later, we're still sitting at the long table. The water bottle is now empty and the granola bars gone. A revolving door of couples have been in to see Mrs. Kravchenko.

The banter continues next door. I wish I could understand what's being discussed.

At a certain point, my spouse refuses to keep guessing how much longer we'll be made to wait. He puts his arm around my shoulder. The wait is grinding. My palms are sweating and my mouth is dry. Albert conjectures we'll soon have some news. I put my head on his shoulder and rub his back.

My eyes wander to the remaining couples in the room. Everyone is off in their own private world.

A stylish Italian couple directly beside us makes a dramatic fashion statement in matching checkered, pleated pants, bright cotton shirts, and wide-lapel jackets. Their hand gestures speak volumes as they spiritedly converse.

A blonde, well-groomed German couple, also seated close by, speaks in soft, quiet tones. They've positioned themselves stiffly on the edge of their chairs, ready to jump once their names are called. Muted wool business attire reflects their serious demeanour. The plush winter jackets on the backs of their chairs have white fur-trimmed collars.

I can't make out where the remaining five or so couples might be from; they are whispering out of reach. Everyone in the room is trying to remain upbeat while stuck in the same long wait.

I play with the simple gold cross hanging from the chain on my dark green sweater. It's strangely wonderful, and embarrassing at the same time, to share a space with so many people who have come with the same purpose in mind.

Throughout the afternoon, various couples are shown a file and photo of a child. Some seem to be looking through several folders in succession after rejecting certain ones.

It's getting late in the day. I'm now impatient and unnerved. Why have other couples been offered to review a child's file while my husband and I have not? Is there a problem with our adoption portfolio, something improperly filled in, or did we possibly exclude a crucial piece of information?

At long last, Sofia quietly enters the room together with a woman whose red hair is pulled tightly back into a bun. Iryna follows behind the redhead, sits directly beside me, and takes my hand.

The adoption facilitator stares purposefully at us. "Please, Albert and Sandra, read this," Sofia states, taking a beige file folder from the red-haired woman and handing it to my husband.

Albert opens the folder. The contents are brief and to the point, presented on one page. Iryna translates: the child's gender; the date, place and time of birth; the birth weight; the name, age, and marital status of the birth mother; the child's medical status; and the location of the children's home. There is no information about the birth father. The health information describes medical conditions and measurements that are unfamiliar to us.

Iryna assures us a Canada-approved physician in Ukraine will verify the child's health status. Behind the sheet of paper, there is a photo of the child at the time of arrival at the children's home.

My husband takes one look at the photograph, covers his eyes with his hand, and breaks down in tears. He's held his breath all day. But now, with the file physically in front of us, we can let go. We're on the verge of meeting a child who could possibly become ours, I'm sure of it.

My lips quiver and my eyes fill with tears as I touch the child's picture. He's tiny, just a few months old at the time of arrival at the children's home in Simferopol, a city in Ukraine's southern Crimea region. The boy has been at the home for over a year, is registered in the Ministry's database as an adoptable child, and is therefore now available for an international adoption.

At this moment, I don't care that other people—strangers—are sharing the room with us. There is such intense emotion racing through my body that I feel my heart might burst out of my chest. I can't understand what such a small, beautiful boy is doing alone in the world without a family to love him. I allow myself to cry out loud. I want to leave for Simferopol immediately!

The door to Mrs. Kravchenko's office swings open. The director appears in the doorway and silently waves my husband and I inside. Iryna follows closely behind. Albert hands me a tissue; I quickly compose myself. Mrs. Kravchenko seems to remember us from the previous day. Iryna translates that the director is satisfied the recommended child is a good match for our family. Mrs. Kravchenko shakes our hands in a congratulatory fashion, walks behind her desk, and sinks into her chair.

She motions for us to sit and speaks for several minutes, her hands clasped and thumbs spinning around one another while her elbows remain on the desk. Through Iryna, we learn the director is telling us that the chosen child meets the requirements of the governmental bodies of the country of residence of the adoptive parents. With Canadian requirements being extremely strict, more time was required for the National Adoption Centre staff to identify an appropriate child.

I can't focus on the remaining translation of Mrs. Kravchenko's words that Iryna is providing. I'm astonished by the dramatic turn of events. The boy's photo is etched in my mind. My only concern is getting to the children's home as quickly as possible to meet him.

My ears unclog as I hear Iryna reveal that we will likely travel to Simferopol in a few days' time, asking if we agree to visit the child shown in the file.

My husband and I look at one another and nod in agreement. "Yes!" Albert shouts, rising from his chair.

Hospital Visit

It's snowing once again in Kyiv. Boris's German sedan is skidding along icy roads in the traffic-clogged city on the way to a meeting with Dr. Bohdan Klymenko. The physician, head of the children's health department at a local hospital, will advise us on the health of the boy we are planning to meet in Simferopol.

Boris speeds across busy lanes of cars and trucks, jostling to pass. He somehow avoids several fender-benders and steers skillfully to prevent impact. We must be late. Otherwise, why would he take such crazy risks? I note to myself that all of the motorists on the road this morning are men.

I mention to Iryna that women drivers are nowhere to be seen.

Iryna and Boris giggle, and joke with each other in Russian or Ukrainian.

Boris then says loudly and slowly in English, "A woman behind the wheel of car is like monkey with toy."

"Excuse me?" I respond.

"It is not commonplace for a woman in Kyiv to be piloting an automobile," Iryna interjects. "We walk everywhere, take public transit, or command a chauffeur. There is no need for a woman to maintain a car in this city."

"I guess that makes sense …" I say, trying to sound accommodating.

"In Canada, I would imagine women commanding cars in major cities is commonplace?" Iryna queries.

"Generally, yes," I confirm. "I got my driver's license as soon as I turned sixteen. Women drivers are everywhere, in every town and city."

Boris laughs. "Problem with monkey is they are known to slip on their own banana peel."

Albert raises his eyebrows; I drop the conversation as I have no idea what Boris is talking about.

I focus on the purpose of the meeting. Sofia has managed to secure an appointment with Dr. Klymenko on short notice. We have to meet with the Kyiv doctor before finalizing our travel plans for Simferopol.

Since the Canadian government will only permit a healthy child to enter the country as an international adoptee (given that healthcare in Canada is publicly funded), we need to commission the Canada-approved physician to travel with us to the children's home and verify the child's health prior to completing the adoption.

Iryna describes the doctor's credentials.

"The physician has assessed many children in Ukrainian children's homes. We are confident Dr. Bohdan is in the best position to judge the health of the child you are considering for adoption."

As we step out of Boris's car, I'm thankful for a safe arrival.

Similar to the National Adoption Centre at the Ministry of Education and Science building, only every third or fourth light in the vast hallway of the hospital is lit, and the brownish-yellow wall colour seems to be a local fixture. The molded ceiling and intricate archways leading to various corridors evoke an earlier era of architectural grandeur. But now the paint is peeling, the walls have holes, and the stone floor is cracked in numerous places. What a shame for such a stately building to lose her luster; there's much to do to rebuild Ukraine.

Two rows of hard-backed metal chairs face one another along the hallway near the physician's office on the hospital's ground floor. Two seats become free after we've stood in the corridor for about an hour. Albert is content to remain in his spot leaning against the wall, book in hand, leaving the newly freed chairs beside him for Iryna and I. The translator casually mentions that Sofia will join us later. I take that as a sign we'll be spending a good part of our day in the foyer.

About three hours in, Albert and I share a granola bar and bottled water. Iryna refuses any food or drink; she's engrossed in her work translating a document for other clients of hers. Resting a clipboard on her lap, she scribbles hastily on a lined paper block. The writing style is jagged and narrow; I notice she rarely makes any corrections.

As my two companions are busy reading or writing, I close my eyes and try to sleep. I quickly realize I can't. Despite being physically and mentally drained from waiting in hallways for days, my mind is racing. I return repeatedly to the description and photo of the boy. Seeing the file of the child washed over me like a bucket of cold water to the face. It's real now, the possibility that we could actually become parents to that little boy!

If only things could move faster, get going sooner, yet Albert and I have zero control over our time here in Ukraine. We are herded from one place to the next, the process advancing drip by drip, leaving us confused as to what will unfold or when. It's evident I need to project composure and confidence so as not to be unmasked as completely unhinged, but how much longer can I project such normality? My body is shivering in the chilly reception area. There's no way to get warm, my nerves are shot, and I want to scream.

How do the people sitting and standing around us remain unflustered? Mothers with small children on their laps wait patiently and silent. A man in heavy work boots cradles a small baby in a blanket. Standing by the wall, he jokes with another man who is with a teenaged boy. These people have all been in the hospital waiting area for hours, same as we have, yet no one seems concerned about the long delay.

In the early afternoon, Sofia enters the corridor in her elegant navy overcoat. She is talking on her mobile phone but quickly snaps it shut when we make eye contact.

"Well, we go to see Dr. Bohdan now," she triumphantly states, taking my arm as I stand up. She ushers us in to the doctor's dark office. I'm grateful Sofia is running the show behind the scenes. Her arrival opens doors.

The sparse doctor's bureau is lit with a diminutive metal table lamp on a smallish desk. An X-ray table beside the desk adds brightness but also gives the room an eerie glow.

Dr. Bohdan stands teetering near the doorway, like a prize fighter who's ready to fall after a nasty bout but somehow remains standing. Tall and rakish, the doctor is nattily attired in a striped gray suit under his white doctor's coat.

"Hello, pleased to meet you," the doctor says in fairly good English, while extending his bony hand to Albert. As he smiles Dr. Bohdan reveals deep wrinkles lining his face.

"Nice to meet you, too. Thank you for seeing us today." Albert shakes the physician's hand enthusiastically.

"It is my great pleasure," Dr. Bohdan retorts. "I have met many families from around the world. Canadians are among my favourite. Your politeness is appreciated."

The physician's graying hair is neatly trimmed. Reaching to shake my hand, he touches the bridge of his wire-rimmed glasses with his other hand to ensure they don't slip off his slender nose.

"Please, take your seats."

Albert and I are shown to two wooden chairs closest to the desk; Sofia and Iryna stand behind us.

Dr. Bohdan sinks down onto the edge of his desk as Sofia hands him the boy's medical file. The physician removes a pen from the inner pocket of his white coat and reviews the medical information on the child we are planning to visit in Simferopol. He rereads the page several times.

"I will need to see this boy myself, as you know," the doctor says, looking at Albert and tapping the page with his pen.

"Yes," my husband says.

"There isn't much to go on, but I have to say, there is nothing here to be alarmed about at this point."

Dr. Bohdan hands the paper back to Sofia, puts the pen back in his pocket, and crosses his arms across his chest.

I wonder what the physician is alluding to, about not being alarmed "at this point." I shuffle my feet beneath the chair and make a move to stand up. Before I can speak, Sofia stops me by pressing her hand down on my shoulder.

"What Dr. Bohdan is saying is please, do not be concerned. The child will be properly evaluated. You will see; everything will be in order."

Sofia squeezes my shoulder. I turn around to see what she wants; her eyes implore me not to speak. Against my natural instinct to question what I don't understand, I stay quiet.

Albert is sitting stone-faced looking straight ahead at the doctor. If he's not concerned about what Dr. Bohdan has said, then I'll leave it at that.

The physician checks his appointment book. He verifies his availability, with the caveat that he can only make the trip if we travel by air, a ninety-minute journey. The twelve-hour train ride to Simferopol is out of the question, as the doctor's work schedule does not allow so much time away.

My husband and I confirm with Sofia that we agree to the request, and Dr. Bohdan circles a departure date on his agenda. He stands up, points to a large map of Ukraine tacked up on his office wall, walks over to it, and touches the spot where Simferopol is located.

"It is slightly more than 800 kilometres south of Kyiv," Dr. Bohdan enlightens us. "I have been to this children's facility a number of times. It is a good one. Well run, with an experienced team of health professionals and caregivers."

Albert thanks Dr. Bohdan for taking on the task. Sofia asks Iryna to book the flights to Simferopol and explains we will all travel together in three days' time.

Albert pays Dr. Bohdan his fee for preparing the assessment on the boy in advance. The receipt is presented in Cyrillic; my husband looks at it for a few seconds, then slips it into the zip pocket of his backpack.

What a relief to get out of the cold hospital and back into Boris' warm car. I'm worried that the constant waiting around in frigid spaces will cause me to fall ill.

Our next stop is the Embassy of Canada. Boris fights his way through the start of the afternoon rush hour. Blocks of boxy apartment complexes, tired and in need of renewal, give way to well-maintained dwellings on tree-lined avenues near the privileged embassy row.

After the security check at the wrought iron front gate of the Embassy of Canada, we are buzzed in to the compound. The stone residence is square and stately. As we enter through a heavy glass and wood door, the embassy's interior presents a typically modern Canadian office with modular beige furniture. I imagine the diplomats who work there feel right at home.

It surprises me how much I'm touched by the maple leaf flags and Canadian insignia throughout the building, the artwork and photos of prime ministers on the walls, and maps of Canada displayed on cloth dividers at employees' workstations.

The lady we meet with at the embassy, Svitlana, is a Ukrainian national, but her command of English is superb. It's nice to be able to speak English so freely for the first time in days with the friendly government official.

I've brought along a chocolate bar that Laryssa, our Toronto adoption agent, asked me to give Svitlana. The woman is acquainted with Laryssa and it's meant to be a small gesture of hello. We've been warned by the Toronto adoption agent not to try and influence or bribe officials in Ukraine in any capacity. Based on Ukraine's recent scandals with black market babies, Laryssa implored us to walk a straight line. As I'm delivering a chocolate bar on behalf of someone else, I don't consider it to be a bribe.

The bureaucrat seems surprised by the gift but graciously accepts the chocolate and quickly puts it away in her desk.

Our business with Svitlana is to register our passports, obtain forms that Dr. Bohdan will need to fill in for the medical assessment of the boy, and start the official proceedings on the Canadian side of preparing papers for the potential arrival of the boy from Simferopol to Canada.

It seems precipitous to my husband and I to begin formal discussions about a child we haven't yet met. However, Sofia explains that since we'll be traveling far to visit the boy, we had best avoid having to fly back and forth between Kyiv and Simferopol to address the various legal and bureaucratic requirements that have to simultaneously occur among Canadian and Ukrainian officials if we wish to move things along in a timely manner with regard to that child.

While in Canada, we'd already applied for and received the appropriate documentation for granting landed immigrant status to a potential child we would adopt from Ukraine. In Kyiv, the next logical step is to prepare the landed immigrant papers that Svitlana will begin to process if we definitively decide to adopt the boy from Simferopol. If we choose not to proceed with that particular child, we would then return to the National Adoption Centre in Kyiv and replay the procedure from the beginning, starting with the initial waiting line for a meeting with Mrs. Kravchenko.

However, Laryssa made it clear to us in Toronto that the first child presented for consideration in Ukraine has been selected with great care by the National Adoption Centre experts based on the parents' adoption file.

Laryssa told us, "You will be matched with one child and, barring any unusual considerations, the first match would ideally be best suited to you and your family. You can restart the process, but it would likely not change much in terms of age or circumstances of the child. Everything is considered according to the file you submitted to Ukraine and aligned to what the Government of Canada demands in relation to health status."

Albert and I are relieved Sofia is thinking ahead and finding ways to save time. We complete the necessary forms, sign them, and let Svitlana know we'll be in touch.

Sightseeing

A plume of cigarette smoke floats out a half-open front window of Boris's car as we exit the Luba hotel. Iryna is in her usual spot in the front seat beside Boris, reading a newspaper.

Climbing in, I notice the bulky blue scarf our translator has draped around her neck. It's a fashionable accent to her overcoat. The citrus-floral perfume or body lotion she's wearing reminds me of spring.

Albert checks his backpack to ensure he's brought along his still photo camera and a city map, although I wonder why he needs a map when Boris and Iryna will be navigating. I watch him close the backpack clasp and turn his attention to the car window.

My husband is serene and relaxed in his black cap, striped black and grey scarf, and dark grey coat. He's ready to take in the sights of Kyiv as they are revealed to us. I'm awed by his calming presence, by his warmth and unconditional love. It's wonderful to experience.

I, too, look forward to a day of sightseeing, touring around in the cocoon of Boris's comfortable sedan. It will be the perfect antidote to the past few days of waiting endlessly in frigid, dark hallways.

Iryna reads out loud in English the weather report for the day: a high of -6°C, sunshine, and high winds.

Boris powers past the Dnipro River and up a hill into the historic part of the city. I can tell it's bitterly cold outside; the car exhaust around us forms large clouds of smoke. The driver abruptly stops in front of an internet cafe on the street level of a large commercial building. Iryna instructs us to get out. She, too, exits the car, and I watch Boris pull away from the curb.

"Where is he going?" I ask, perturbed.

"Boris will be back at the end of the day," Iryna responds. "We are touring the city on foot. Please, come inside the cafe for a moment. I must send an email; perhaps you would like to check your emails, too, Sandra and Albert?"

After we read and respond to emails from family, friends and work colleagues, Iryna leads us on a marathon hike through the centre of Kyiv.

She describes the city as a cosmopolitan, historic jewel built on a series of hills with the Dnipro River dramatically dividing it in half. I imagine Iryna must have been a tour guide in previous years, as her descriptions of the city are highly detailed and absorbing.

We trek to Saint Sophia's Cathedral, a massive and imposing church with numerous gold domes and an exquisite interior of Byzantine frescoes and mosaics. The edifice is surrounded by a large open square and is opposite St. Michael's Monastery, an ancient religious complex of brilliant blue hues with a series of gold domes and vividly decorated arches.

Everywhere in Kyiv, there are beautiful churches to admire. Albert enthusiastically snaps photos of these beautiful places of worship.

From St. Michael's, we head to the Golden Gate, a huge, medieval stone structure that was the city's ancient entrance and fortifying wall dating back to 1017. We stroll down Andreevsky Spusk, a steep, curvy cobblestone street where local artists sell religious icons, cultural souvenirs of embroidered linens and hand-painted ceramics, newly painted cityscapes, and humorous wooden Matrushka dolls painted with the faces of Russia's Vladimir Putin and American president, Bill Clinton.

We trudge a short distance up a hill that reveals the Baroque exterior of St. Andrew's church, a gigantic house of worship fashioned by a Russian imperial architect. The spectacular columns and green domes of the intricate edifice are finished with crosses soaring high atop the building.

Iryna schools us, teaching us that the spiritual heart of Kyiv is being beautifully restored following the neglect of religious structures under the Soviet regime. We stop at several high points on streets where we can see expansive city vistas. My husband snaps more photos.

We walk for hours. Our translator rebuffs all offers to stop for lunch or a hot beverage, saying we only have a short time to see Kyiv and it's important to squeeze in as many sights as possible so that we can gain an understanding of the city's rich cultural history. It amazes me that the woman practically never puts food into her mouth. There is no question, Iryna is exceptionally slender, which would account for the lack of eating, but where does she get all her energy?

Iryna peppers our tour with historic facts about the city. Kyiv, and Ukraine itself, has long been ruled by foreign regimes, the longest of which still holds tremendous sway in present times. Russian culture and language dominate daily life in many parts of the country. Ukrainians are split about the meaning of their national identity.

Taras Shevchenko, a famous Ukrainian poet, writer, artist and political figure, looms tall as a statue across the street from the university. But in every part of Kyiv, from street vendors to restaurant owners and business people, Iryna acknowledges Russian is the language most frequently heard. Many native Russian speakers live in Kyiv, and native Ukrainian speakers are fluent in Russian because they learned the language in school. (After Soviet leader Joseph Stalin ordered the murder of millions of Ukrainians in the 1930s, he imported millions of Russian speakers into Ukraine to make Russian the dominant language.)

Albert and I glance knowingly at each other. We understand what Iryna is talking about. Every time we've visited Riga, Latvia, Russian is the prevailing language heard. From retail stores to banks, eateries and other commercial enterprises, Russian speakers abound. As a Latvian speaker from the West, it's difficult to understand such disrespect for a country's official language. We've been asked to leave establishments in Riga when we demanded service in Latvian, and, in the end, I'm happy we did not spend our money in places where Latvia's nationhood is belittled.

It's nearing the end of the day, and getting bitingly cold. I'm grossly underdressed in my short car coat, thin sweater, and plaid wool skirt. My feet are sore from blisters which have formed on my toes from trudging too long in high-heeled boots. I can't understand why Iryna and Albert won't take a break to warm up; they both want to keep sightseeing. My husband is clearly in his element in Kyiv, enjoying the brisk outdoor air and soaking up historic places of interest, but I've had enough.

The sun is disappearing from the horizon, and workers are pouring out into the wide boulevards to head home. Turn-of-the-century street lamps cast a romantic glow on the meandering, sloped streets. Neon signs light up shops and restaurants. A light snow is falling, covering the cobblestone sidewalks.

I anxiously await Boris' arrival. I assume that at any moment Iryna will pick up her mobile, call him, and he will magically appear to return us to our hotel. Nevertheless, Iryna has other plans.

The translator checks her wristwatch. It's nearly 18:00. She suggests we walk a few more blocks to a restaurant for a quick dinner, as she's purchased tickets for my husband and I to see the evening performance of the Kyiv Ballet. The ballet is being presented at the Taras Shevchenko National Opera and Ballet Theatre which is only about a half an hour walk from the restaurant. I want to return to the hotel because I'm freezing cold and tired. Instead, I smile sweetly at our tour guide.

Thankfully, the restaurant is a self-serve cafeteria, offering fresh salads, grilled potatoes, boiled and pan-fried cabbage, and assorted shish kebabs for instant gratification. We grab a table and proceed to the food counter. Albert and I gulp down a substantial meal of cabbage rolls, as we are famished.

Iryna sips a small bowl of vegetable soup and has cottage cheese for dessert.

As we climb a series of massive stone stairs, the opera and ballet house has a striking design with a large, curved roof and Neo-Renaissance arches. The round, classical interior hall and performance theatre are immaculately maintained. For the first time all day, I'm glad to be wearing my fancy boots and feminine tartan wool skirt, as most of the patrons are elegantly attired.

The Kyiv Ballet performs selections from *Romeo and Juliet* and *Carmen*. Emaciated dancers in intricate costumes pirouette and leap with grace against a simple dark blue backdrop. Normally a loyal fan of the ballet, I have trouble paying attention. In my mind, I'm already in Simferopol about to meet the little boy. His photo calls out to me. I try to imagine how and where we'll meet, what I might say to the boy, and how he'll react to the encounter.

When Boris pulls his car up in front of the steps of the opera and ballet house after the performance, I nearly weep with joy.

"Boris! Please, to the Luba hotel!"

******

On our final day in Kyiv, Albert and I are provided a tour of the Kyiv Pechersk Lavra, known as the birth place of Orthodox Christianity and the most sacred monastery in Eastern Europe. It's a gigantic complex of ancient churches, monastery buildings, and a bell tower that dominates the city's skyline. A series of underground caves contain the centuries old, mummified Orthodox priests' remains.

My husband is itching to visit the site, as religious history is one of his passions. He verifies that his camera battery is charged and that all his photographic equipment is in his backpack. I watch him staring dreamily out the car window on the way to the Lavra.

I push my arm deep into my handbag to make sure I've packed bottled water, granola bars, and hand wipes, as we may not see the inside of an eating establishment for most of the day. I've also brought along some toilet paper that we transported from Canada. On the rare occasions in Kyiv where we've been presented with a public toilet, such a facility is usually a tiny closet with a hole in the ground and a large rope hanging from the ceiling that you pull to flush once everything is done. You have to quickly jump up onto two ceramic ledges installed at the sides of the inner stall when flushing, otherwise the water floods your feet. There's never any toilet paper or sink in which to wash up.

I'm assuming the sorry state of public toilets is a vestige from the days of Russian occupation. Latvia's lavatory situation was eerily similar, until recently, when the country upgraded its public lavatories, particularly in Riga, to approximate Western standards.

We're to be joined at the Lavra by an American-Canadian couple also in Kyiv to complete an international adoption. Iryna reveals that the couple will travel with us to Simferopol. I'm torn about the prospect of making polite conversation with strangers about our own plans.

Over the past year, the adoption preparations consumed me. The expectation of sharing our adoption journey with people we don't know is a bit daunting.

Albert rebuffs my concerns and chastises me for being reluctant to socialize. He reminds me, the consultants are doing their best to keep us entertained and upbeat before the long slog of administrative and judicial hurdles that lie ahead. I button my coat all the way to the top as my husband helps me out of the car.

Prior to the Ukraine trip, Laryssa, our Toronto adoption agent, mentioned two clothing taboos for travel in the country: jeans and athletic shoes. She underscored the need to "dress respectfully" wherever we go.

I imagine that Ukrainians, like other Europeans, save their jeans and athletic wear for weekend outings at a country home and they don't parade around in them right in the heart of a major city.

Among those assembled at the wrought iron entrance to the Lavra, are two people sporting jeans, white sneakers and blue ski jackets. As we near the duo, they smile amiably at us and wave.

"The North Americans," I mutter to Albert under my breath.

"Hi there!", the woman says.

"Hello." Albert's tone is cheerful.

"Nice to meet you," the man says, introducing himself as John. His handshake is steady.

I try to sound enthusiastic. "Lovely to meet you."

The grinning woman with big white teeth is Mary. She hails from the United States, and John from Canada, but they now live in Berlin. I'm a bit taken aback that the couple are so friendly, telling us with great sincerity that it's wonderful to meet another couple in Ukraine who are on the same path as them.

"Let us know if there's anything we can help you with," Mary chimes in. "We're all in the same boat."

Try as I may, I have no reason to criticize the North Americans. They're compassionate, open and approachable, like many of our compatriots.

Boris and Iryna speed off in the car. An English-speaking tour guide is provided to us inside the monastery grounds.

The chain-smoking guide is a little man with a pock-marked face. His English description of the monastery buildings and monuments is precise and grammatically correct, but if you ask him anything unrelated to the site, he begins to stutter and doesn't seem to understand the question.

The monastery buildings and underground caves cover several kilometres. Apart from being a major tourist attraction, the Lavra is the official residence of the current head of the Orthodox Church and a functioning religious site. The opulent, gold-encrusted buildings have been painstakingly restored down to their intricate elements and are awe-inspiring to see. Albert turns to excitedly inform me that the Lavra is a testament to the continuing strength of the Ukrainian Orthodox faith.

A couple of hours into the tour, I'm relieved to learn that Mary and John are eager to venture down into the caves to see the mummified priests' remains. I know my husband wants to view them as well, and that means I'm off the hook. An earlier visit to the Catacombs of Paris, home to the crypts of famous French writers and composers and a place used by Nazi Germany to torture World War Two French resistance fighters, makes me reluctant to repeat a similar claustrophobic underground experience.

The tour guide shows me to a nearby chapel, and explains that the group will come up from the depths of the caves in about an hour. He'll return to collect me at that time.

I push open the large gilded doors of the chapel and step inside the vestibule. Glancing deep into the interior of the church, no other visitors are present. The chapel is dark; a row of candles burns in front of an elaborate altar. Frescoes on the walls depict stories from the Bible.

Turning back, I take a look around the vestibule. My eyes are drawn up toward the curved ceiling to an ethereal pink, white, and gold fresco of baby angels. The angels' faces mesmerize me. They gaze down directly at me, serene and beautiful with their white feather wings, as they float among puffy clouds.

Seating myself on a wooden bench, my eyes return to the angels. This is it; I have to come clean with the angels. I married a man with three daughters, who rightly deserve parental love, supportive presence and guidance. I knew I was in way over my head when I tried to create a role for myself with Albert's girls. Working long hours as an executive at a public relations firm, I barely had the energy to manage my own life, let alone provide any help to my husband in raising his daughters. Less than two years after we married, I left the firm to do part-time, freelance work. The reality of family life caught up with me.

Is it selfish to add a fourth child in our home? Are we putting too much pressure on a family that is already overflowing with commitments to work, school, and community?

I drink in the stillness of the vestibule.

I'm comforted by the thought of our large extended family at home in Toronto and beyond waiting to shower a new child with love. My stepdaughters are thriving. One more girl or boy in the house will only strengthen the family bonds.

And, apart from everything else, Albert and I are here in Ukraine because we decided together that we want to raise our own child.

I need to live the whole experience of motherhood. Dress my child in the morning. Help them eat. Teach them to speak, read, and sing. Walk them to school. Read them bedtime stories. Hold them when they're frightened by a dream or can't sleep and have tough conversations about life when they're old enough to tell me where to go. I want it all, the unbridled joy of raising a small human being to adulthood and supporting them in whatever they need as long as I live.

Do the angels hear me? Will they respond? I look up again; there is only silence and a faint smell of burning candles.

The vestibule is starting to feel warm. The angels are communing with me; I know they're telling me a child has been chosen for Albert and I to cherish.

"Thank goodness," I say. "How much longer were you going to make me wait?"

I remain in the chapel and watch the angels dance.

Eventually, the tour group resurfaces from the caves. The guide comes to collect me. Albert describes animatedly in detail the leathery hands and long nails of the mummy priests' remains and the arduous walk down and back up the rickety underground staircase. I'm glad to have been spared the experience of the cramped cave system.

It's late afternoon. John and Mary propose, and we agree to, a short walk through the city towards a restaurant for dinner they recommend called Saigon.

The eatery, with its red and gold Asian decor and two distinct menus, one Vietnamese cuisine and the other Ukrainian, is delightful. The pho, with its beef, noodles, and vegetables in rich broth, hits the spot.

John and Mary reveal they've visited Kyiv several times. Travelling together with us to Simferopol, they are in the process of completing approvals on a girl and boy they've previously met and agreed to adopt. Both children reside in the same children's home as the boy we'll soon meet.

My feathers are initially ruffled that we'll be part of a large delegation of people descending upon Simferopol. But then I realize that our adoption facilitator, Sofia, in her wisdom, has used her head behind the scenes. She's arranged for Dr. Bohdan to review the medical status of the child we'll visit as well as finalize documents and procedures for the children John and Mary are adopting. This will allow us to share hotel, flight, and meal expenses for the doctor and for our translator and facilitator.

John and Mary explain that they have travelled extensively through Europe. The small inconveniences of a post-Soviet state don't seem to annoy them. They could not care less about the lack of takeaway coffee in Kyiv or spotless public toilets. As the couple are renting a centrally located apartment in Kyiv for their stay, I assume they can always pop in to their apartment should a sudden need arise.

Language is also not a barrier. John speaks passable Russian and offers to assist Albert in ordering the right brands of beer and vodka at meal times.

"In Crimea, where we're headed tomorrow," John reveals, "everybody speaks Russian. Only government workers would need to use Ukrainian, because their jobs demand it."

After dinner, the pair invite us to join them for "pub night" at the Embassy of Canada, where John has close contacts. Albert and I happily tag along and take advantage of the opportunity to let off steam and consume several rounds of beer and wine.

At the embassy social, we meet a stylish blonde woman from Canada who reveals she is acquainted with Sofia. The woman owns a successful Toronto bakery and collaborates with our facilitator on fundraising initiatives for children's causes in Ukraine. She praises Sofia's dedication and verifies we're in good hands.

Nearing midnight, my husband and I hobble clumsily back into the Luba hotel elevator and press twelve to be transported upstairs.

At the twelfth-floor landing, Albert satisfies the male concierge that we are legitimate guests, and we are allowed through.

Instead of ducking left to go down the long passageway to our room, we foolishly head right. Part way down the corridor, we see a staircase leading a few steps downward. We follow the stairs and discover a full hallway of rooms which are essentially between the eleventh and twelfth floors.

"A secret hallway with hidden rooms!" my husband mischievously declares. "This is where the Russian spies, or Ukrainian secret service, are holed up. I wonder if they've found a Latvian language speaker to monitor the conversations in our guest room?"

"Ha, ha. Let's get out of here," I say, shaking my head. "Our room is the other way."

Crimea

A handful of Italian hunters in felt hats and long rubber boots hoist gun cases and carry caged dogs at their sides in the departure lounge of a Kyiv commuter airport. Their back-slapping antics and roaring laughter provide comic relief to our anxious circumstances of not knowing whether we'll be allowed to travel on the flight we've booked to Simferopol.

Our translator is negotiating with a ticket counter representative who's given her three tickets less than were reserved for our group. No more seats are available on the plane, Iryna tells us. The next flight out is in three days' time.

The translator is so visibly distressed her body is contorted. She politely tries to explain the situation to the woman behind the counter. All of us must be on today's flight, as we have urgent meetings with government officials and children's home representatives in Crimea.

I nudge Albert to try and resolve the dispute. He lifts his hand, showing me "stop" with his palm, indicating "no."

"What can I do?" he crows. "The clerk doesn't understand English and I don't speak Ukrainian or Russian. Let Iryna handle it. We're paying her to take care of things. The flight

SANDRA UPESLACIS

is obviously overbooked; there's nothing new in that. Airlines play games to ensure every seat on a flight is used. Iryna will work her magic and we'll get out on time."

My husband retrieves an historical novel about German theologian, Martin Luther, from his backpack, sinks into a chair, puts on his glasses, and starts to read.

I look to Mary. I can tell she agrees something needs to be done. But her husband, too, has walked away and won't get involved. Mary nods at me and points to John, signaling she will work on getting him to do something.

Dr. Bohdan stays put on his chair in the lounge, head buried in a newspaper. Sofia is speaking on her cell phone while walking around the terminal.

Twenty minutes before our flight is due to leave, John rises, yawns, and stretches his arms. Albert glances up from his book, puts it away, and follows John to the ticket counter, where Iryna is still negotiating our departure. The trio returns shortly with a full complement of tickets, allowing our party to travel together. Iryna's face is beet red.

My husband explains to me in Latvian that while the economy section was apparently overbooked, there were plenty of first-class tickets available on the flight, but Iryna didn't think she had the authority to buy them. As the first-class fare for each ticket to Simferopol costs $40 USD, compared to $26 for economy, John and Albert immediately paid the additional amount for three first-class tickets so everyone in our party could fly.

My husband instructs Iryna not to be deterred by cost. Travel and accommodation in Ukraine are extremely afford-able for those traveling on American dollars, and we all agree the plan is to do whatever is necessary to bring our children home as quickly as possible.

The Soviet era airplane, which literally looks to be held together with duct tape, sputters as we march on the tarmac. The engine is loud; we can't hear Iryna's instructions. The Italian hunters with their caged dogs and gun cases are wandering chaotically around the outside of the plane, evidently trying to figure out how they will board with all their paraphernalia. A flight attendant is arguing with the group.

Iryna tries to tell us something, but we can't understand her instructions above the noise. She lifts her suitcase and demonstrates we need to put our own bags into the belly of the plane. We quickly see there isn't enough room for everyone's luggage. A flight attendant takes the bags we can't squeeze into the luggage compartment, gestures for us to get in, and shoves our bags behind the pilot seats in the cockpit.

We board the plane. Everyone in our group is seated in first class, save for Iryna. Albert offers to change seats with her but the translator refuses, saying she prefers some time alone.

The difference between first class and economy is not significant, as the seats are all the same size. Economy seats face forward. Rows of first-class seats face each other, and in between them are wooden card tables screwed into the floor, allowing passengers to read, eat, or drink in a group.

The Italian hunters are last to board the plane. All of their barking dogs have been allowed inside the passenger area. The dog cages miraculously fit underneath the hunters' seats. I assume the gun cases have been locked away somewhere.

"This should be interesting," my husband says, chuckling. "There's no need for an in-flight movie; we can listen to the soundtrack of *101 Dalmatians* playing behind us."

The takeoff is brisk. After a short time, a flight attendant comes around with a jingly trolley filled with assorted beverages in tall, slender glasses and bottles. Passengers beside us order glasses filled with what appears to be water, so we point to request the same. John smiles playfully. Once I put the glass to my lips, I realize the beverage is vodka, not water.

"How do you say 'water' in Russian?" I ask John.

"*Voda.*"

The next time the flight attendant comes by, I ask for *voda*.

She doesn't have any, so I point to what looks like a bubbly orange drink and the attendant gives it to me. I take a sip; the beverage is thankfully non-alcoholic.

The flight to Simferopol passes quickly, despite the dog chorus serenading passengers from the back of the plane. The propeller plane slowly descends. There's a marked change in topography from Kyiv. Crimea's southern geography has abundant green vegetation.

As we exit the glass and steel terminal building, the sun is beginning to set in bright pink and orange hues.

Sofia is approached by two tanned and fit men sporting leather jackets. Our consultants exchange double-cheeked kisses with them. The tall one, Yevgeny, is introduced as our chauffeur.

We walk to the parking lot. Yevgeny helps place our luggage, along with Dr. Bohdan's, into the trunk of his sedan, and signals for the three of us to get in.

The other man, Viktor, slightly older and heavier set, is acquainted with Mary and John from their previous visit. Sofia explains he will once again drive them around Simferopol. Mary, John, Sofia, and Iryna climb in to Viktor's car.

I roll down my passenger side window and inhale the fresh breeze. It's fragrantly scented with notes of eucalyptus and cedar. The temperature is warmer than frosty Kyiv. I try to stretch my legs but there's not much room in the vehicle.

When Yevgeny hits the gas, I immediately start thinking about the little boy in the children's home. How soon can we visit him? Is the home far away? How will we manage our first meeting? I compose my thoughts while the driver speeds along several curved cobblestone roads toward the centre of the ancient town. There are numerous potholes, but Yevgeny evades them, as if by memory. Albert's camera clicks away.

The car lurches up a street with a steep incline then pulls sharply to the right into a laneway and stops at a metal gate. We've arrived at a hotel called Svoboda. I lean forward in the back seat and look through the front windshield beyond the gate. Ahead is a white, four-storey building with a brown tiled roof. The guest rooms have balconies and there's an adjoining, lower-level hall. The property is dotted with trees and shrubs. It would be a lovely place for a summer vacation, I decide.

Sofia steps out of Viktor's car, which has stopped beside ours. She ambles to the speaker at the entrance gate, hits the buzzer, and announces our arrival. After several minutes of talking into the speaker, Sofia walks back to the car and gets in. The electronic gate buzzes loudly and opens unhurriedly. Viktor drives through, with Yevgeny following. Several cars and trucks are stationed in the outdoor parking lot.

The Svoboda is smaller and has more of a resort feel than the formal Luba hotel in Kyiv. I can't see any Ukrainian armed forces personnel patrolling the property. The atmosphere seems relaxed.

"Where are the soldiers?" I ask my husband.

"The Ukrainian military is not going to flex its muscles here, in Simferopol, when Kuchma is sitting on his throne in Kyiv," he explains to me.

I'm somewhat confused but drop the conversation.

Inside the hotel, two middle-aged ladies behind a tall wood-paneled reception desk busy themselves with reviewing our party's passports and discussing the room requirements with our local team. Something is amiss. Iryna and one of the reception staff are together scrutinizing a faxed piece of paper the translator has retrieved from her oversize handbag. The other clerk counts and fingers a number of keys in cubbyholes on the wall behind her.

The woman reviewing the paper with Iryna turns to engage her co-worker. Sofia gently proposes that the rest of our group takes a step outside for some air.

Mary and John are first out the door; Albert and I follow. Dr. Bohdan shuffles from behind, lighting a cigarette. He leans against the exterior wall of the hotel, rubbing his eyes. Sofia and Iryna are left to do their job.

"Hah, it's just how they do business here," John smirks. "The last time we were in Simferopol, we stayed at a different hotel, the Palace, just down the hill. It was the same story. You book a certain number of rooms, confirm with a fax, and when you arrive for check-in they say, 'Sorry, the reservation was an error,' or 'was lost,' or something to that effect. Then you show them your reservation, plead, beg, and negotiate, and eventually you get a room key."

My husband and I decide to explore the grounds. The black pine trees and leafy bushes bordering the hotel are tall and aromatic. We follow a path through the greenery on one side of the property that leads to an opening above the steep, paved road we took to get up the hill.

The motorway is ridden with potholes, some so wide and deep if you fell in, you'd likely die. Albert cautions me to avoid them and holds my hand tightly as we move down the hill. There's a busy commercial street at the bottom. It's unclear how we might cross to the other side. With a rush of cars to contend with, we decide against going any further. We hike back up the hill to the hotel. In the parking lot, our party remains outside. I'm beginning to wonder if everything in Ukraine will be a lengthy negotiation.

After much debate with the front desk ladies, Iryna joins us outside. She tells us one member of our group will have to take a business class room, which costs a few American dollars more per night than the other guest rooms. John and Albert instantly agree that Dr. Bohdan should take the upgraded room, given that he will be staying the least number of nights and has come all this way to help us. They remind Iryna that a few dollars here or there are insignificant to us in the grand scheme of things, and that cost should not deter her from completing a transaction.

The Kyiv doctor initially declines the superior quarters, as he does not want to take advantage of our generosity, but upon John's insistence, Dr. Bohdan relents. I'm perturbed as to what the fuss is about. It's clear I have no understanding of the value of a few American dollars to someone living in Ukraine.

The Svoboda does not have an elevator, so we trek three floors up to our room, suitcases in hand. John and Mary are assigned the room next to ours.

Once my husband figures out how to open the door with its finicky lock, we enter a bright and expansive guest room. Its pastel pink and blue furnishings and wall coverings provide a whimsical feel. Large windows reveal the lush greenery extending far beyond our hotel. A door leads to a balcony. The guest room has a sitting area with comfy chairs and a television. A kitchenette with sink, stove, and refrigerator is installed along one wall. At the other end of the room is a double bed, and off the bedroom area, a small bathroom with a shower stall.

Given that we may possibly be staying a month or more in Simferopol, I'm pleased with the accommodations.

I lift the receiver of the telephone perched on the television set to see if it works. The line is dead.

"We should let the front desk know our phone needs to be fixed," I tell my husband.

"Okay."

We don't have much time to unpack our belongings. John has recommended meeting in the lobby within an hour for dinner out at the nearby Palace hotel. He and Mary enjoyed past meals at the Palace's restaurant and tell us the menu is reasonably priced.

Albert retreats to the balcony to take some photos of the surrounding area.

I unpack our suitcases, arrange our toiletries in the bathroom, and tuck our clothes away in a large wooden dresser near the bed.

My task complete, I turn to Albert. "Hey, I'm changing into something nice for the restaurant; you can take more shots later. We shouldn't keep the others waiting," I say.

"I'll be right in."

I pair a blue silk blouse with my black wool slacks, as I want to enjoy the ritual of a night out. My husband removes his cashmere sweater and opts for a button-down, striped cotton shirt. We comb our hair, brush our teeth, and head out. I'm happy I had my hair cut in a short, easy-to-maintain style before the trip.

Leaving the room, Albert curses the door lock; the key is stuck. He jiggles and wiggles the key in the mechanism until it finally pops out.

Our group travels gingerly down the steep hill from the Svoboda to the commercial street below. John leads the way with a flashlight, as the sky is now completely dark and there are no working street lights. Albert holds my hand tightly and positions himself slightly ahead of me, ensuring neither of us ends up in one of the formidable potholes. Dr. Bohdan supports Sofia and Iryna in navigating the terrain. There are no sidewalks; a passing car could easily hit us if we aren't careful.

At the bottom of the hill, John points to an illuminated pedestrian crossing. We walk up the road a short distance and cross. A few hundred meters away is the vertical landmark of the Palace hotel, an imposing edifice with nearly 200 rooms, some of which cast light upon the dark street. A gaudy neon roof sign in Cyrillic script announces the hotel. A square stone overhang, tilting upward, shelters the main entrance. Tall evergreens, cedars and spruces border the property.

I suppose the Palace was once a popular spot for vacationing Soviet elites as it's one of only a handful of hotels in the city. Simferopol is the lone entry point to the seaside resort town of Yalta, famous for revitalizing sanitoriums, spa treatments, vivid nightlife, and a tropical beach setting full of palm trees and bougainvillea. It was no secret that Russian czars, and the Soviet strongmen who followed them, loved to holiday on the Black Sea, about an hour's shuttle ride south of Simferopol.

Yalta was also the fateful location for the wartime conference of 1945 between American President Franklin Delano Roosevelt, British Prime Minister Winston Churchill, and Soviet Premier Joseph Stalin. That meeting brutally changed the face of Europe after World War Two, handing the Soviets control of much of Europe for half a century.

As an ethnic Latvian, I have deep sorrow about the disastrous Yalta Conference. The Soviet Union was never held accountable for the many atrocities committed against the populations of the countries the Russians invaded during the war and annexed as a result.

Apart from devastating Latvia's cities and countryside, the Soviet Union carried out forced deportations in 1941 and 1945–1951, resulting in 60,000 Latvian adults and children being sent to inhospitable, remote areas of the Soviet Union. The deportations from Latvia of June 14, 1941, when 15,000 people were forcibly deported in one day, are forever imprinted in the memory of every ethnic Latvian.

Since the earliest days of my childhood, I remember Latvians around the world marking June 14 as a horrific, solemn reminder of Soviet aggression. Out of the June 14 deportees, thousands died in exile, on the journey or by execution. For a country with a total population of just two million people, losing tens of thousands of its civilians through forced displacement and murder by a conquering army is an outrage and, by today's standards, a gross violation of international law.

(Meanwhile, Germany admitted responsibility for its actions in World War Two, acknowledged the atrocities it had committed, reconciled with Nazi victims, and made reparations.)

"Watch your step," John advises as we traverse unevenly positioned stones at the Palace hotel entrance.

We enter a spacious, dimly lit hotel lobby. John exchanges a few words in Russian with a young man behind the reception counter and heads toward the right side of the room.

Turning around to face us, John says, "Follow me."

To reach the restaurant, we pass through a door on the right wall of the lobby which leads to a gambling hall, and beyond that, through another door, to a billiards room thick with smoke. A handful of men in tidy slacks, white shirts, and black suspenders hold beer glasses and joke around, cigarettes dangling from their mouths.

John shows us to a third door we need to step through at the back of the smoky room, which finally leads to the main restaurant.

"Are we in a James Bond movie?" Albert jokes. "Do they actually want people to find the restaurant?"

"There's another entrance; I'll show you next time," John responds. "The restaurant will be worth it, trust me." He slowly pushes the heavy wooden door inward and holds it open for our party to enter.

The Baroque-themed Palace dining hall is a visual delight, evoking old-world grandeur. Giant wood beams, sumptuous accents, floor-to-ceiling, burgundy velvet curtains, intricate chandeliers, and precious tapestries provide an inviting ambiance.

The venue is in fact a huge supper club with discreet private booths. A small stage in one corner has a silver disco ball suspended high above it. Microphones and audio equipment are strewn about the stage area.

The seven of us slide into a circular, high-backed booth. The oversize velvet seating is comfy and luxurious.

Our elegant server, Anatoly, introduces himself with a deep bow. His black tuxedo is frayed at the edges, but his command of English is excellent, and his manner, refined. The man remarks on his forty years of service in the establishment and confidently asserts we have chosen the best place to eat in all of Simferopol. John agrees, thanking Anatoly for the previous meals he and Mary enjoyed at the Palace.

The menu is extensive and, as luck would have it, printed in several languages, including English. Assorted varieties of marinated, smoked, and grilled fish, spicy meats, cabbage, grilled vegetables, and a potpourri of potato offerings beckon. Anatoly meticulously explains the intricacies of particular dishes, and scribbles down our dinner selections.

"Excellent choices," he exclaims, smiling widely.

For beverages, John proposes vodka shots to start, followed by local organic beer. He discourages our group from consuming any of the wines on the menu as his past experience warns against it. Albert and Dr. Bohdan join John for the vodka shots; the rest of us order tea.

John raises his glass to make a toast.

"Let me take a moment to say it's a pleasure to share a meal with all of you here tonight in Simferopol. Sofia, Iryna, and Dr. Bohdan, thank you for everything you've done so far, in helping Mary and I move towards finalizing the adoption of our two wonderful children. We've waited a long time, and we'll wait a little more. Then it will be a new life for the four of us! Albert and Sandra, your journey is well under way, and I wish you all the best."

"Thanks, John. Cheers! To new beginnings!" Albert clinks his water glass against John's.

"Yes, to new beginnings," Dr. Bohdan adds, lifting his vodka shot.

I'm happy to have met John and Mary. They will be good company, sharing a parallel journey to ours in Simferopol, and John's command of Russian will surely come in handy.

Once we consume the beverages, Anatoly discreetly appears at our table to let us know the meals will take a while longer to prepare as there is a small problem in the kitchen.

Given that we are the only patrons in the restaurant, we joke amongst our party that the chef probably has to dash out and purchase provisions for what we ordered so that the kitchen staff can prepare the dishes. Sofia and Iryna are poker-faced.

Dr. Bohdan proceeds to enlighten us about his travels throughout Ukraine. He's visited children's homes all over the country and has seen extreme poverty, malnutrition, and challenging living conditions up close. But the physician adores the children he encounters and believes it's his duty to protect them.

"Much of the time, there is no medicine to treat even a simple ailment. A case of the flu means a children's home is quarantined to prevent further spread. A respiratory infection in a child could prove fatal."

At the same time, Dr. Bohdan notes many positive changes have been occurring in Ukraine's children's homes since the country regained her independence in 1991. Some are doing really well. Donations are pouring in from around the world of food, medical supplies, and money to improve the physical infrastructure of the buildings. More and more families are adopting children. There is real hope alongside the struggles, Dr. Bohdan insists, downing his glass.

Although the food service is slow, the meal does not disappoint. Albert delights in his succulent grilled salmon with root vegetables, and I devour my chicken Kyiv lathered in butter, garlic, and parsley served with roast potatoes. Dinner has a discernable calming effect.

Following the heavy meal, we inch laboriously back up the hill toward the Svoboda, our stomachs full and our hearts content to have enjoyed an evening out with fascinating company.

Back in our guest room, my husband clicks on the TV. Miraculously, it works. Even better, there is a channel in English, broadcasting the BBC World News.

"Can you believe it? It's the BBC!" Albert shouts excitedly.

I try the phone receiver again. Thankfully, there's a dial tone.

I ready for bed, climb in, and watch my husband catch up on international news. The guest room is chilly. I touch the radiator beside the bed. It's cold. I scurry out of bed, find an extra blanket in a cupboard by the wall, lay it on the bed, and get back in.

Having taken some important first steps in Ukraine toward expanding our family, I'm relieved and happy things have gone well so far.

Week Two

Yolochka

Sunlight streams into our Simferopol guest room through a large gap in the heavy curtains covering the windows along the balcony and bedroom area.

Rising from bed, my first priority is to bathe. Careful not to wake my husband, I tiptoe to the bathroom. When my foot touches the frigid, ceramic tiled floor I'm reminded the heat in the guest room is off. A hot shower will do the trick.

I turn the large silver handle in the stall down and to the right, the only direction it will move. Water comes gushing out, but it's freezing cold. I wait a minute or so, letting the water run, hoping it will warm up. No such luck. Another minute. Still cold.

I brace myself for a quick soak. Turning the water on and off between soaping, shampooing and rinsing, I race through

the bathing ritual, shivering. Just as I've completed the final rinse, the water becomes lukewarm. I let it run some more. It gets warmer, then scalding hot. I jump out to avoid getting burned.

"Now that's ridiculous!" I yell, unintentionally rousing Albert.

"Huh?" His voice is raspy.

"Quick. Come and have your shower," I call out. "I've warmed up the water for you. It's either freezing cold or boiling hot. There's no other way to wash here."

Albert kisses me directly on the lips and tickles my sides. "Well, good morning to you too!" he purrs.

"You've got plenty of time to get ready, but let's make sure we're not late meeting Mary and John."

"Got it; thanks for heating up the shower."

I dress, arrange my handbag to ensure we have the required documents for the day, and pull back the curtains of our room to reveal a bright, sunny day. Stepping out onto the balcony, the vista from the hilltop hotel is postcard perfect. Rows of tall cedars, towering pines and spruces, and bright flowering bushes blanket the expansive view against a brilliant blue sky.

"It's lovely here, so peaceful." I step back inside.

"Yes, it is," Albert agrees, getting dressed after his shower.

My husband fiddles with the key outside our hotel room once again as we seek to leave for breakfast. The key is weighty, fashioned out of metal, and stuck in the keyhole. After much turning and twisting, it finally loosens, comes out, and Albert verifies that the door is locked. Mary and John have already left their room and stand patiently in the hall waiting for us.

We take the stone stairs down to the lobby, and gesture to the women at the front desk with our hands that we're off to eat.

"I'm famished," I tell my husband.

"Me too."

A server in a black dress and white apron balances a platter of breakfast orders on her shoulder. Her back is rigid; she floats effortlessly between the tables, not allowing the large weight to slip from her slender arms.

The Svoboda dining room is alive with the clatter of dishes and chatter of guests. A savory aroma from the kitchen rouses my taste buds. I hear some Americans at the table next to ours talking about their missionary work with the poor. A group of Poles nearby are scouring a hunting map of Crimea.

Our table is on a raised level near the kitchen, which seems to be the warmest place in the eatery. Faint music plays from a radio deep inside the kitchen.

A server places breakfast plates down in front of us. She mentions something about chai that I take to mean someone will be around to pour tea.

Soon, a server glides around with pots of tea, pouring black chai into small cups. There's no milk or cream to be had, but sugar is plentiful in small ceramic pots on the tables.

Breakfast consists of shaved cabbage in vinegar, boiled rice, and hearty pork stew. Some guests at other tables have fried eggs on their plates or eat porridge out of shallow bowls. I point to the other meals and try to make the servers understand we'd prefer something else. A harried server rattles something off in Russian or Ukrainian, and disappears.

John offers to sort things out with the dining room staff, but before he can, four big breakfasts are dropped down in front of us. It becomes apparent why the Ukrainian doctor, translator, and facilitator are skipping the meal. Who can eat such heavy food in the morning?

The jovial Poles dig in to their stewed pork and cabbage and swiftly clean their plates. The Americans sip chai and push the hefty meat entrees to the side of their table.

After breakfast, John, Mary, Dr. Bohdan and their driver leave for the children's home, as the Canadian-American couple are further along in the adoption process than my spouse and I are and have already been granted visitation rights to their daughter and son.

Albert and I wait outside the hotel for the rest of our group to arrive. Sofia and Iryna soon appear, looking ready to do business in chic suits, coiffed hair, and dramatic makeup. I marvel at the sparkly jewel decorations on Sofia's high-heeled, black patent leather shoes.

We head to an appointment at the Simferopol town council. Leafy trees line historic boulevards and cobblestone sidewalks along the drive. Intricate stone and wood facades reflect the kaleidoscope of influences in the region, from ancient Greek to Turkish, Islamic, Byzantine, and Rococo.

It's the morning rush hour. Pedestrians are hurrying to work in long coats with briefcases and plastic shopping bags at their sides. Cars, trams, and buses roar past us in every direction. The city has a liveliness that is palpable.

Simferopol was erected on the site of a fifteenth century Tatar settlement. It was the former administrative centre of the Independent Republic of Crimea and therefore had a vaulted status in the region. It's the second-largest city in Crimea, with more than 300,000 residents, and it is a hub of economic, cultural, and regional government activity. Some parts of the historic centre, including the grand railway terminal, have been restored to their former splendour.

Crimean Tatars were an ethnic minority in Ukraine that was forcibly deported to Central Asia by Soviet dictator Joseph Stalin in 1944. Stalin falsely accused the Tatars of collaborating with the Nazis. Nearly half of the 200,000 deportees loaded onto freight cars died on the journey. Following Ukraine's recently regained independence the Tatars began returning to the area.

Our morning meeting is with the managing director of the city's children's services office in a local administration building. We are there to obtain an official document allowing us to enter the grounds of the children's home to visit the child identified for our consideration by the National Adoption Centre at the Ministry of Education and Science in Kyiv.

Albert has brought along his Martin Luther historical novel to read in the hallway outside the director's office while we wait. I have my notebook and pen to scribble thoughts and impressions about our adoption trip. We are now accustomed to the notion that a nine o'clock meeting in Ukraine with a government official will possibly materialize at some point later in the day, but likely not at the specifically designated time.

Our Ukrainian consultants begin their work day by making what seems to be an assortment of sweet-sounding compliments to the clerk in the room adjacent to the director's office. The woman doesn't budge. We're told to join the hallway line up.

Other people already in the queue are patiently waiting their turn, and appear well accustomed to doing it. In Soviet times people in occupied European countries stood in line for hours each day to buy food, household products and other basic necessities. The system worked for decades. Why change it? Who needs a welcoming waiting room with chairs to sit on when people are willing to stand outside in the hall? Maybe Canadians have it wrong. Is it inconsiderate to expect a comfortable waiting room and prompt service from a government official?

For the first time in days, I'm battle-ready and relaxed in comfortable flat shoes and warm woolen slacks. I'm neither cold nor so exhausted that I want to lie down. It's going to be an important day, and I have to be ready to think on my feet, respond to any questions, and seize every opportunity to move things in the right direction. I'm hoping Albert and I will finally meet the little boy!

Shortly before noon, we are escorted into the director's modest, airless office. A dour woman sits ramrod straight behind her desk, back against the wall. A carved wooden table lamp illuminates the appointment book on her desk. Nervously, I make eye contact with the lady and smile.

She glares back at me as if to say, "You idiot, why are you smiling at me?"

I wish I could respond in perfect Ukrainian, "You're the idiot, I'm showing you respect by smiling at you. Would you prefer a scowl?"

Iryna instructs us to take a chair.

The administrator is attired in a dull, manly suit. I conjecture her demeanor is purposely gruff because she wants to intimidate us.

The inquisition begins. The lady focuses her attention on my husband and asks why we have come all the way from Canada to take one of Ukraine's beloved children out of the country. Are we planning to raise the child ourselves, or do we have other motives?

Albert sits with a blank facial expression, hands clasped together on his lap. He seems shocked by the question. The woman peers icily at him; my husband's eyelids flutter but he doesn't instantly respond. I can tell the gears in his head are turning as he formulates an answer. The bureaucrat is growing impatient.

I reach into my handbag and pull out the family photo album we compiled and brought along on the trip. My hand is trembling as I open it; the lady has managed to throw us off balance. I place the album carefully on the desk and begin turning the pages.

"Ah, this is a photograph of our home in Canada," I explain. "This is the bedroom we have prepared for the child."

Iryna is translating.

"We would like to meet the child that the National Adoption Centre in Kyiv assigned us to visit. We have approval from your government, and from Canada."

The woman slaps the desk hard with a wooden ruler and blurts some words out over mine. Iryna grabs my arm and tells me to stop speaking.

"The children's services director wants Albert to do the talking, as he is the head of the family," Iryna clarifies.

My husband's cheeks become flushed. He retrieves his reading glasses from his jacket pocket, leans forward and takes the photo album out of my hands. He calmly proceeds to show the woman some photographs.

"These are my three daughters," Albert begins, clearing his throat. "Here we are celebrating my youngest daughter's birthday. This is a photo of our backyard."

The lady challenges my husband to prove the legitimacy of the adoption. He decisively refers her to our voluminous adoption file, which Iryna has brought along. The woman takes it, looks through some of the pages, and hands the file back to the translator.

I don't like the tone of the prodding questions the director is asking about our home, the kind of car we drive, our financial status, whether or not we fear God, and why on earth we would want to adopt a specific child from Simferopol that we have never even met.

I compel myself to stay quiet. Albert holds his ground.

After about an hour, the inquisition is completed. My husband has successfully prevented the town bureaucrat from beating him into a pulp. He's answered every question to her satisfaction. I touch the back of my husband's shirt; it's soaked with sweat.

The children's services director signs the required form, stamps it, and hands it to Albert. She stands to shake his hand, but ignores me. I don't take it personally. Iryna motions for us to leave, and we do.

Heading to the car, Sofia clarifies in a near whisper that many adoption directors and other professionals working in the children's sector are wary of adoptive parents' intentions, because rumours abound in Ukraine of children being adopted in order to harvest their organs for transplant purposes.

"Please, keep this information confidential," Sofia warns us, her voice now growing louder. "Do not repeat this to anyone."

Yevgeny drops us off at an Uzbek restaurant for lunch in the city to kill time before our late afternoon appointment at the children's home. Iryna joins us for the meal, but Sofia stays in the car, as she has other business to conduct in town.

I'm pleasantly surprised the restaurant is heated and the washroom has a fully functioning, clean toilet, a sink with a mirror, and toilet paper. I feel dirty after the long wait at the children's services office and use the opportunity to wash my hands with soap and warm water and comb my hair.

Glancing in the mirror, I'm taken aback by the ashen pallor of my face. I brush on rouge to brighten my cheeks, comb and tease my hair, and put on lipstick. It wouldn't hurt to spend some time outside in the Simferopol sun, I tell myself.

The Uzbek diner doubles as a gaming arcade. Electronic consoles cover much of the wall space. Roaring car motors, squealing tires, and cheering spectator sounds provide unique background noise while a group of teenagers eagerly race on mock Formula One tracks.

Iryna recommends we order a hearty soup called *solyanka*. It's thick and spicy, full of smoked meat, pickles, vegetables, and dill. The concoction is delicious, but Iryna manages to swallow only a few spoons' worth. The server brings us full cups each of "instant coffee" after the meal; it's how coffee is presented on the menu. A glass of milk is provided separately, as we've asked for milk in our coffee.

I'm about to ask Iryna to outline the procedure that is customary for visits to the children's home when Sofia races in to the restaurant to get us.

"Please. Can we take care of the bill? We must leave *now*."

Yevgeny's car zooms through town. I roll down my window. The sun is out and the sky is luminous blue. The winding roads, blossoming vegetation, and pastel buildings along the route remind me of homes in the south of France, despite the fact that many of Simferopol's edifices are crumbling or in various states of disrepair. Kiosks on selected street corners and houses with bright shuttered windows show promising signs of rebirth.

The sedan turns down a laneway and comes to an abrupt stop in front of a big wire gate. Beyond that is an expansive garden with pine and spruce trees, rose bushes, and a curved driveway. At the edge of the driveway stands a rectangular, low-rise building. The surrounding property is enormous.

"*Yolochka*," Yevgeny declares.

"It is the name of the children's home," Iryna explains. "It means 'pine tree.' This is in relation to the adjacent forest."

Sofia gets out of the car and walks over to the gate. She presses a button on a metal box and announces our arrival, then returns to the car and climbs back in. As the gate opens wide, Yevgeny drives through.

The air is cool and aromatic when we step out of the car near the main entrance. Three black-and-white cats scamper away as we near the building. Gravel crunches under my feet. The large treed property is a serene and inviting place for a child to roam. But at Yolochka, there are no children outside, and no young voices can be heard in the distance.

About 200 children live in the home, Iryna informs us, infants and toddlers up to age three. At age three, if a child has not been adopted, they are moved to another children's home and remain there until age six. Every three years, a move would be made to the next age-appropriate place. On their sixteenth birthday, a child is released from state care and left to fend for themselves. Literally.

I try to calmly absorb the information about what happens to children who are never adopted, but I'm brought to my knees. How can some children in the world be in a position where no one is ever willing to take them in? What kind of world are we living in?

The heavy metal main entrance door creaks and slams shut loudly as we step into the sizeable foyer. An elderly lady swaddled in layers of well-worn sweaters and a dark wool cap runs the front reception desk. She bows her head respectfully to Sofia and Iryna and they exchange a few words. When Iryna tells my husband and I to take a seat on the wobbly chairs near the front door, the administrator cranks her neck to look in our direction.

The lobby is painted pale green, a welcome change from the yellow-brown halls of Kyiv government buildings. But there are large gaps and cracks in the tiled floor, and the walls have numerous chips and holes that need more than just a new paint job. A bare light bulb hangs askance from the ceiling, suspended by black and gold exposed wires. Luckily, the building's entrance has a large window adjacent to the main door that allows natural light to fill the space.

Sofia opens her purse and presents the administrator with our stamped papers from the town council. The old lady gingerly lifts her eyeglasses; they are held together with masking tape. She carefully reviews the document, nods, and hands the papers back.

Flipping through an appointment book on her desk, the administrator stops at a page where her arthritic index finger touches a specific entry. She stares at the entry as she lifts the telephone receiver on the desk and slowly punches in a number.

Sofia removes her overcoat and recommends we do the same. She alerts Dr. Bohdan of our arrival on her cell phone. He appears momentarily in the reception area from within the children's home compound.

A while later, a side door to the lobby opens; a man in a grey suit enters the foyer.

"You can go now," Iryna says. "The gentleman here is the head physician at Yolochka."

Dr. Bohdan is first to shake hands with the man. The two of them appear to know one another and converse quietly as Albert and I follow the duo down a vast, dark hallway. We encounter several women in white lab coats moving silently in pairs along the corridor in our direction. None of them smile or nod to acknowledge us.

All of the doors along the way are closed. As most of the ceiling lamps are not working, and there are no windows, it's hard to make out where we're going. I listen for children's voices as we move past each door, but there aren't any. There are no carriages, playthings, or children's shoes to be seen, nor can I hear any music, laughter, or giggles.

We turn down another long, dark hallway, pass more closed doors, go all the way to the end, and hike up a concrete stairway to the second level.

The second floor is identical to the first—dark, silent, and oppressive—and there doesn't seem to be a working heating system in the building.

We stop at a narrow wooden door. The head physician unlocks it with a key, shows us inside, and gestures for us to take a seat.

I remove my coat. My bottom sinks into a low, well-worn, Scandinavian chair. I cover my legs with my coat to keep warm. Albert takes the chair directly beside mine.

I scan the room. There's a stethoscope on top of a wooden desk, a locked medicine cabinet with a glass door bolted high on the wall, some poster diagrams of the human body taped to the wall, and a television set with rabbit antennas on a small table at the opposite end of the space. I guess we've been brought to the head physician's office.

Some brief words are exchanged between the two doctors, and the children's home physician leaves the room.

"Dr. Bohdan, what's going on?" I ask.

"Please, be patient," he replies. Dr. Bohdan then removes his suit jacket and places it on the back of one of the chairs in front of the desk. He lifts his medical bag up and onto the desk, unfastens the clasp on the bag, and places his arm inside.

Albert plays with his reading glasses while Dr. Bohdan pulls his arm out of the bag, snaps the bag shut, straightens his tie, and sits down on a chair in front of the desk.

The three of us wait silently. The faint ticking of a clock somewhere in the room is driving me bonkers, as I can't figure out where it's coming from. There are no visible clocks or timepieces anywhere.

The stillness of the space becomes claustrophobic. My husband and I exchange nervous glances. Albert smiles at me in the sweetest way he knows, encouraging me and urging me not to worry.

We're about to meet the little boy, I'm certain. I want to savour the moment, to remember it forever. I summon my courage and fight the urge to cry.

I study every frayed thread in the carpet on the floor, count the medicine bottles in the high cabinet, and stare at the posters on the wall. My eyes follow the maze that is a diagram of the human intestine. *How utterly uninteresting*, I think to myself.

The door creaks open and a plump blonde woman in a white lab coat walks in, cradling a small boy on her elbow. The child is terrified. He keeps his head buried deep in the lady's chest, arms tucked under his chin.

The toddler is less than two metres away, but I dare not approach him. I don't want to frighten him even more.

The woman sits down with the boy in her arms on the chair beside Dr. Bohdan's. He introduces her to us as Natasha, one of the caregivers for children in room S-11. When the caregiver smiles at us, she reveals a smooth gold cap on one of her front teeth.

Dr. Bohdan stands up, straightens the belt on his pants, and shakes Natasha's hand. He then steps back and observes the child interacting with his caregiver. The woman whispers something softly to the boy, but the child keeps his head close against her chest.

After a moment or two, Dr. Bohdan appears to be gently asking the toddler to show himself. He won't. Dr. Bohdan repeats the request, his voice becoming sweet and higher pitched than usual.

The caregiver again whispers to the child. The boy briefly lifts his head from the woman's chest, revealing himself to the doctor. His eyes are red from crying. He grabs the lapels of the lady's white coat with both hands and digs his head back in.

The child is pale and shockingly thin, with slight wisps of blond hair. He looks small for a sixteen-month-old. A bony face accentuates his almond-shaped, gray eyes. The child's large sweater is secured at the waist with a flannel pajama belt; the sleeves are rolled up to match the length of his frail arms. The toddler's tiny legs nearly disappear in wide-leg pants, and the socks on his feet are mismatched.

Dr. Bohdan speaks softly and kindly to the child. He strokes his head back and forth, showing him there's nothing to fear. The boy finally turns toward the physician, allowing Dr. Bohdan to fully see him. I'm surprised by the lack of expression in the child's face. He stares blankly into space.

My eyes are glued to the little boy's every move. I want to scoop him up in my arms and tell him that all will be well. I see the hope and misery etched on his face, a quiet dignity despite everything. I believe what the child most urgently needs is to be loved. I want to touch him, but I don't want to startle him.

Dr. Bohdan calmly discusses the child with Natasha. She recounts all kinds of information. I keep my eyes on the little fellow. His face remains expressionless.

The Yolochka head doctor returns to the room and quietly takes a seat on his chair behind the desk.

Dr. Bohdan opens a file folder and the two physicians review it together. Dr. Bohdan scribbles some notes on a piece of paper.

I don't know if it's appropriate to smile at the caregiver after the experience with the cantankerous town council lady. But this woman's face is sympathetic; she smiles at us with her eyes. Albert and I beam back at her. I try to remember some words in Russian I've previously heard. All I can come up with is, "*Zima prishla*. Winter has arrived."

It was a phrase my father learned as a boy in his native Latvia. Natasha's eyes light up. She starts conversing with us enthusiastically. We stare nervously back at her. I feel bad that I don't know what she's saying. I repeat the phrase, "Winter is here," and she then understands that we don't really know any Russian.

The child calms down a bit. Dr. Bohdan takes him from Natasha's lap, slowly removes his sweater, shirt, and undershirt, and sits him on the edge of the desk, all the while talking to the child. The toddler's ribs are prominent on his chalk-white, gaunt torso.

Dr. Bohdan places a stethoscope against the child's heart, determines the circumference of his head with measuring tape, and examines his stomach, back and limbs. He places the boy down on the carpet and watches him stand up and walk around. The toddler does what he is told.

With a nod of Dr. Bohdan's head, the caregiver takes the child's hand and dresses him once again in his pajamas.

Dr. Bohdan turns to my husband and I. He stares intently at us and waits before speaking as if to say "Please pay attention; this is important."

"Albert and Sandra, this child will be fine. He needs a family, a home, people who will love him and care for him." I sense the genuine concern of the doctor, who obviously has a soft spot in his heart for the little boy.

Dr. Bohdan folds the piece of paper he's been writing on and puts it into his medical bag. He gently takes the child's hand and walks him closer to where my husband and I are seated. The doctor points to us, crouches down beside the toddler, and tickles his stomach to try and get him to smile, but the child refuses to look in our direction. I want to reach out, hug the boy, and tell him he has no reason to be sad or afraid, but the child is naturally uncomfortable in the presence of strangers.

Dr. Bohdan lifts a developmental toy that we've brought with us from Canada out from his bag, and shows the child how the square blocks fit into square holes, the round ones into round holes, rectangles into rectangular holes, and triangles in triangular holes. He hands a square block to the toddler and encourages him to put it in the right hole.

The little boy's face lights up a bit as he holds the bright red block in his hand. He inspects it from all angles, relishing the feel of it in his delicate hands.

Dr. Bohdan asks the child to place the block in the correct hole. The little fellow isn't listening; he's fascinated by the block in his tiny hand and keeps staring at it, turning it over and over between his fingers and palms.

The physician again urges the child to drop the block into the appropriate hole. The boy brings the block directly above the right hole, but refuses to throw it in.

"Why would I drop the block into the hole when I would then lose it?" the child evidently is thinking. He is looking directly at Dr. Bohdan. "I will not relinquish the block," the child is saying with his eyes.

After repeated prodding from the Kyiv physician, the toddler lets go of the square piece and it drops into the appropriate hole. His face is now inconsolable. He turns toward Natasha and reaches his arms out to her. She returns the child to her lap and he digs his face in deep against her chest.

Moments later, the child and Natasha are gone. My husband and I are dismissed and escorted back outside to wait in Yevgeny's car while Sofia and the others conclude their business at the children's home.

******

John and Mary are patrolling the Svoboda main lobby when we return. Sofia, Dr. Bohdan, and Iryna quietly glide past us, heading into a small cafe a few steps up the main stairway and to the left off the lobby.

"Well? How was the little boy you met?" John inquires.

"Oh! He was incredibly sweet, shy, sad, and frail," I blurt out. "It's overwhelming. We're both very emotional. What else could we expect?"

"We signed up for this," Albert joins in. "We had an idea of how things could unfold and can't say we didn't know. So now we have to show courage to see where it leads us."

"Good for you!" Mary is grinning.

Our compatriots have cause for celebration. Medical clearance for their children is now in process.

John wants our whole group to return to the Palace hotel for a dinner celebration. Mary beams proudly beside him. I notice her Gap sweatshirt has a stain across the right shoulder; I don't have the heart to tell her, and it's likely she doesn't care.

"Give us fifteen minutes, and we'll be back down," Albert responds.

We race up to the third floor. My husband nearly screams when he has to wrestle with our guest room key again, but I tell him it's just nervous energy he's feeling from the day, encouraging him to turn and nudge the key a little slower. Eventually, the door unlocks. We change into less formal clothes, put on comfortable shoes, and head back to the lobby to meet our dinner companions.

John practically pirouettes his way down the treacherous hill behind our hotel, pulling his wife's hand behind him while she tries to keep up and maintain her balance. Albert and I try to match John's quick pace, but Dr. Bohdan, Sofia, and Iryna take their time walking carefully down to the street below.

I don't mind dining at the Palace again, although I wonder how to justify such gluttony in the face of the children's home conditions Dr. Bohdan described and that we just witnessed.

We can't drive back to the home and suddenly provide enough food for the 200 children living there who need it. We can donate some money and food, but whatever we offer won't be enough to feed all of them, and it won't sustain them over time. We can only bring one child home; that is what we agreed to and what we are legally allowed to do. So, I have to reflect on what happened today, how exhilarating and heartbreaking it was to meet the little boy, and go deep inside my heart and head to consider what my husband and I should do next. Given that the price per person for dinner at the Palace is cheaper than a fast food meal in Toronto, we can't in all honesty turn John down.

Ensconced once again in our booth at the restaurant, Mary orders assorted appetizers and insists we all try them. There's a caviar crepe with sour cream; sliced avocados atop a shrimp and egg salad drizzled with lime vinaigrette; and smoked salmon with pickled onions on dark rye bread. Anatoly, the waiter, is pleased with Mary's choices and promises the main courses, too, will be satisfying.

John orders a round of beer. Dr. Bohdan adds a vodka shot to the order. Mary and I join the men for a beer; and Sofia and Iryna opt for mango juice.

Everything is delicious. Mary gushes about how well their children are doing.

"This is our second stay in Simferopol, and while we've only seen our kids for a short time this trip, they're progressing nicely and are growing closer to us," Mary reveals.

"When I think back to the first time John and I met them, both of our children could not walk unassisted. They were very hungry and small for their ages. They never had enough to eat, so when we fed them on our visits, they ate everything we offered them. It's tough when we have to leave our daughter and son at the children's home after spending time together, but it won't be for long now."

Dr. Bohdan adds, "It is amazing to watch how the children develop with the patient care of parents. Language is not a problem; they pick it up quickly. Despite the fact that they're very young, they know full well what is going on. Every child at Yolochka is waiting for a family; that's essentially what they are doing all day. It's normal for a child to want to be cared for, to have parents who love them. I wish we could grant every girl and boy at Yolochka this opportunity, but of course many will not be so lucky."

The physician downs his vodka.

Anatoly returns to our table several times to calmly state the main courses will arrive momentarily. By the time the dishes are served, I've come down from the day's adrenalin rush and feel hungry. We dig into pork roast in mushroom sauce with grilled carrots and beet salad. Iryna has passed on a main course and headed straight for vanilla ice cream with chocolate sauce, followed by Siberian herbal tea. John and Dr. Bohdan top off their meal with Russian cognac. Albert is too satiated to join them.

On the way back up the hill, we switch positions. The three Ukrainians march in front with us North Americans in back. The trio is deep in conversation.

Back in the silence of our Svoboda guest room, the day's gripping experiences are beginning to sink in. I try to absorb what's happened. My husband and I got permission from the Town of Simferopol to visit a beautiful little boy. We met him. He's tiny and vulnerable and scared. He won't make eye contact with me or with Albert, and his face lacks expression.

On the other hand, in the exchange with Dr. Bohdan, it was clear the child was communicating to the physician that he didn't want to lose the toy block he'd been given despite knowing which hole it needed to be dropped in. He understood the physician's request; he knew where the block should go, but wanted to hold on to it as long as possible. He was thinking and acting appropriately. Like any clear-minded youngster, the boy was reluctant to give up a toy, but when prodded, complied. I felt bad when he had to give back the block.

Dr. Bohdan said the child is healthy and simply needs a family to love him. Is that true? Is that all we need to know? Will the boy be able to bond with us as parents and with his three sisters as siblings? Why were Albert and I permitted only a few brief minutes with the child and then quickly ushered out of the children's home?

Despite the late hour, it's impossible to sleep after the visit to Yolochka. How exhilarating and excruciating it is that we finally met a child who could conceivably become our son. My heart unquestionably opened wide, but we need to be absolutely certain we're headed in the right direction.

Albert and I toss and turn and shiver in the discomfort of our unheated hotel room. The night is frigid. A biting wind whistles through large gaps in the window beside the bed, and the window frame repeatedly flaps against the ledge.

We agree that the experience of meeting the little boy was far more difficult than we'd imagined. We've been introduced to a shy, courageous child who needs parents, who is all by himself in a Ukrainian government-run facility, but we can't reach out to him … yet.

I use up a box of tissues trying to pull myself together.

After scouring the cupboards for more bed covers, I find an old woolen blanket on a high shelf to spread out on the bed. When I shut my eyes, I can't drift off. I keep seeing the child's face and his tiny body. I rise again and pull on my thermal socks, hoping to finally warm up and get some sleep.

My husband tires of my constant shuffling and fidgeting. He gets out of bed and clicks on the television to watch BBC news. There is a story about the Florida recount in the American federal election, with no decision yet on George Bush versus Al Gore for president. Mad cow disease is gripping Germany. Apparently, nothing important is happening in Canada, as it doesn't warrant a mention.

In my mind, I'm back at Yolochka, in the dimly lit room with the child who has stolen my heart.

My husband is as emotionally charged as I am. We hold each other and cry. We agree that we urgently need to see the little toddler again and we want some information clarified. We hope Dr. Bohdan can reaffirm his good health.

The hours between night and day pass like a slow, dense fog that I can't make my way through. I know my heart is beating, but my body is heavy and immovable. If only the sun would rise, the weighty burden pushing down on me could lift.

The Child

Finally, morning.

My head is pounding as my husband and I enter the Svoboda hotel dining hall for breakfast. Dr. Bohdan is seated alone at a table. The rest of our group is absent.

"Good morning," the physician greets us.

"Hello." Albert's voice is raspy.

Dr. Bohdan peers up from his newspaper. He watches us take the chairs beside him, then neatly folds the pages of his paper and places it beside his breakfast plate. He removes his wire spectacles, rubs his eyes, and positions the eyeglasses delicately back on his nose. He can read in our faces what's up. We haven't slept a wink and worried all night about the little boy.

The physician calmly sips his tea and assures us the child will likely pass the Canadian medical examination. He offers to return to the children's home with us that very morning, finalize his assessment, and put his personal stamp of approval on the toddler. Dr. Bohdan can't guarantee that the Canadian government official based in Vienna who will review the child's file will concur with his recommendation, but he shares there's

SANDRA UPESLACIS

nothing in the boy's history or his latest physical examination that would suggest the official would not do so.

"It is for the most part a formality," the doctor says. "Your government wants to know that the child entering Canada is in good health. In my opinion, the boy we met yesterday meets the criteria. I have evaluated many, many children, as you know. Your toddler is doing well, all things considered."

What exactly does Dr. Bohdan mean by "all things considered?"

It's on the tip of my tongue, the rant that is about to come hurtling out of my mouth, but I'm determined not to embarrass Dr. Bohdan nor denigrate his country for not having adequate resources to look after its vulnerable children. I make a superhuman effort to shut up and radiate tranquility.

It's obvious to everyone that the child we met is malnourished and likely neglected or possibly even mistreated, given that his face is blank and impassive. What kind of place is Yolochka? Why call it a "home" for children when it doesn't look anything like a home and there are no children anywhere to be seen?

People in white lab coats and serious suits move noiselessly through unheated rooms and halls, ruling with what appears to be an iron fist. How else do you explain the soundless, dark, foreboding place where children's voices are silenced?

Dr. Bohdan doesn't need to hear the pain in my voice. He's obviously taken it on the chin from countless other foreign couples long before my husband and I showed up in his country. He's had plenty of opportunity to let the reality of life for orphaned and abandoned children in Ukraine eat away at him. Albert and I are new to the system, temporary pawns in a much larger game, but the physician lives with his truth, day in and day out. Anything I say will only aggravate the situation.

I drink my chai tea in silence.

******

The black-and-white cats at the children's home are sprawled on the front steps, soaking up some sun as we arrive in Yevgeny's car. One of the cats meows and runs away when Dr. Bohdan, my husband, and I approach the main entrance.

We cross the threshold and the heavy metal door slams abruptly behind us, nearly clipping my hand. The elderly front desk administrator scolds us and pulls her dark cap down low over her ears. I suppose the draftiness of the room, with the frequent opening and closing of the main door, makes her disagreeable. Dr. Bohdan exchanges some words with the lady in what sounds to be Russian. The administrator shrugs and shows us to the shaky chairs by the door.

We remove our overcoats and sit down. Dr. Bohdan retrieves from his jacket pocket the piece of paper he had written on the day before when we met the little child. He unfolds the paper and reads it. Seated beside Dr. Bohdan, I try to stealthily make sense of the text, but it is a series of indecipherable Cyrillic scrawls. Albert taps my arm and frowns at me, letting me know he does not approve of me trying to read the physician's private notes.

We are ushered by a lady in a white lab coat down the long, dismal hallway on the main level. The only perceptible noise is the sound of our heels hitting the concrete floor. Identical to the previous day, each door we pass is silent. At the end of the first hall, we turn left, march down another dim passageway, and then turn right down a third which leads to a white door on the left marked S-11. The woman in the lab coat tells us to wait in the anteroom. She shuts the door behind her.

The smallish room is bright and airy, thanks to a large window above an exit door. Two rows of teeny-tiny shoes and boots are stacked neatly against the wall, and racks of small winter jackets hang in a crisscross pattern on hooks.

Natasha, the caregiver we met in the doctor's office on the previous day, appears in the doorway from an interior room. She motions with her hand for us to wait. A few moments later she returns, holding the little boy in her arms. He seems slighter than I remember, and less agitated than on the previous afternoon.

The child stares vacantly at us. He is wearing tights, beige wool shorts, and a long-sleeved navy fleece top with a Winnie the Pooh graphic. The top could also be a dress as it has a ruffled pink hem.

Dr. Bohdan asks to hold the child. He takes him from Natasha; the boy doesn't resist. Dr. Bohdan carries him around the anteroom, speaking softly and showing the child some hanging hooks, a mounted mirror, the image of a rabbit painted on the wall, and what appear to be names on a sheet of paper tacked to the wall.

The doctor allows the child to feel with his hands the raised velveteen stripe in the room's wallpaper. The boy runs his hands slowly up and down the plush stripe. He's docile and lets the physician do his job. I notice the toddler's perfect fingers and thumbs. Four slender fingers and a thumb on each hand.

Dr. Bohdan returns the boy to Natasha and they chat. I'm fixated on the child's face, subtly trying to get his attention, but he only looks into his caregiver's eyes. He follows her conversation with the doctor. Dr. Bohdan thanks Natasha and turns to let us know he has completed the assessment; all is well. The final document with his signature will be faxed to Sofia. We are to stay with the child and spend some time with him. Dr. Bohdan needs to catch his scheduled return flight back to Kyiv later that day. Natasha will prepare the boy. We thank Dr. Bohdan for all of his help and kind support, and he leaves.

Natasha sits the child on a counter above a shelf with cubby holes. She places a pair of tight, ill-fitting shoes on his feet, dresses him in a puffy pink jacket, and puts a matching pink hat on his head. The caregiver instructs Albert and I to hold the toddler so that he doesn't tumble down; at least that is what I surmise she is saying. My husband and I protect the little boy from falling and follow his every move.

Natasha unfolds a stroller by the wall, puts the child into the carriage and secures it. She unlocks the door leading outside and motions for us to take the toddler outdoors.

Albert carefully maneuvers the stroller down a few steps to the ground. He pushes the buggy forward. We wander the exterior of the building, looking for a good place to spend some time alone with the child. The sun has warmed the air, and birds are chirping around us.

We come across a large wooden sandbox in a wooded area at the back of the home and some climbing gear. Behind that is a verdant forest.

Albert stops pushing the stroller. The little boy starts wailing.

I rush to help the child out of the stroller and pick him up in my arms. He is feather-light and screaming.

My husband is trying to formulate the best approach. "Okay, now. Just a minute …"

I tell the toddler in Latvian that he doesn't have to be afraid, that we're there to play together. Albert strokes his head while I try to soothe him with a hug. The child keeps frantically looking around, angling his head in every direction away from me, squirming in my arms. I put him down on the ground. He stands there, frozen, staring at us, then starts bawling again.

Albert tears his backpack off his shoulders, reaches in, and quickly grabs something to calm the child. "See? This is a … pen! It clicks! Do you hear it? Click, click!"

The young child is transfixed for a moment by the writing instrument. He stretches out his arm as if to grasp it, then drops the arm straight down by his side and wails again.

I slowly inch closer to the child, reaching my arms down trying to pick him up. He walks backward, away from me. The down-turned lip is inconsolable.

"Let him be," my husband says.

We speak to the child in soft voices and try to explain that we are all getting to know one another. It is a ridiculous attempt at conversation because neither my husband nor I speak Russian. The little boy is obviously horrified, wondering who these people are that have taken him out of the only home he knows and are now talking to him in a language he doesn't understand.

"Don't you know *any* Russian?" I ask my husband.

"*Nyet*," he responds.

The child is miserable and keeps looking away, but we continue to speak softly with him, trying to calm him. Eventually, he allows Albert to put him back in the carriage. We find that as long as the buggy is moving the toddler doesn't cry. We walk the circumference of the Yolochka grounds several times.

After a while, a woman in a white lab coat with a sweater over her shoulders approaches us and signals with her hands that we need to take the child back inside. We return to the home through the appropriate side door, into the anteroom of S-11, where Natasha is awaiting our return.

I lift the child out of the stroller, kiss his face and hug him. I so wish we could stay longer. It's disheartening to have to leave after such a short visit; the little boy is incredibly sweet and timid. We came all the way from Canada and we've barely been given any time to spend with him …

The child stares at my husband and I, still with the down-turned lip, questioning our motives. At least he's finally willing to look at us. Albert takes the toddler's hand and tells him it was wonderful to visit with him. I catch my husband fighting tears.

Natasha extends her arms and swiftly takes the boy from me. How awful to have the child ripped away, so matter-of-factly. I watch her remove the young boy's jacket, shoes, and hat, then whisk him away, back into the secret room where he lives. The door shuts behind her.

My husband and I wind silently back through the maze of dark hallways to the entrance of the children's home.

I wonder if the horrible feeling of loss I now have will disappear. Or is it only the beginning of things to come?

One of the resident cats meows very loudly as we exit the building, reminding me of Toronto, where our gray-and-white cat rules our home. My heart lifts a bit.

Yevgeny is in the front parking area, leaning against his automobile, having a smoke. He looks tough in his black leather jacket and dark sunglasses. I presume he could rescue us from a bad situation, should one arise.

"Hotel?" he says, emphasizing the "h."

"No. Internet cafe?"

"*Da.*"

Yevgeny delivers us to the edge of a pedestrian district in Simferopol where cars are prohibited. He parks his sedan in a nearby lot and walks with us through the first block of the commercial area to direct us to an internet cafe. He points to his watch, asking Albert to propose what time we need to be retrieved. My husband lifts three fingers, showing we need three hours of time to conduct some personal affairs, and touches Yevgeny's watch to confirm he should meet us in front of the cafe at 16:00.

Yevgeny indicates his understanding. "*Da.*"

I check my handbag to ensure I've brought disposable hand wipes, and thank goodness, I have. The internet cafe, a few steps down from street level, is brighter and cleaner than the place we visited in Kyiv. However, given that the customers are once again mostly teenaged males, the room emits a foul mixture of perspiration, nicotine, and semen. I can't figure out if the stench is so pronounced because the adolescents don't bathe frequently enough, or if teenage hormones are to blame for the distinctively putrid stink.

I wipe down the keyboard, mouse, and general desk area of the computer we've chosen to use, and take a seat to check my email messages. I reply to each one and type an email home to our extended family. Once that's sent, Albert reads his work emails, takes some time responding to them, and sends an email to his daughters.

We now have less than two hours remaining before Yevgeny will fetch us.

"Let's explore the area for a bit," Albert suggests. "We need some fresh air and exercise to clear our heads."

"Yeah."

Simferopol's commercial district has a Western European feel. Walk-up clothing boutiques are squeezed in among perfumeries and skin care stores offering Italian, French, and German brands. Local cafes display tantalizing menus. All of the commercial spaces have floor-to-ceiling windows overlooking the pedestrian walkway. Families are out strolling in chic European garments.

At a nearby green grocer, we buy some cheese, yoghurt, and juice to store in our hotel refrigerator. Given the short time we have to explore the vicinity, we agree to return for future visits.

Strolling through the district, we observe people going about their daily routine. Men in tailored wool suits walk briskly past us, leather bags hoisted diagonally over their shoulders. Long wool scarves are twirled several times around their necks. Mothers and grandparents hold children's hands as they walk them home from school, backpacks in tow. Girls in pigtails skip excitedly while sharing details of their day. A threesome of boys proudly carries multicoloured soccer balls, eyes wide as they recount funny stories to each other and laugh, open-mouthed.

Making our way back toward Yevgeny's car, my husband and I stop for a moment.

"Are we absolutely sure about what we want to do?" Albert asks, taking my arm and looking straight at me. "Do you agree that we'll adopt the little boy we met from the Yolochka children's home?"

There's no doubt in my mind. "Yes! There's only one way forward. If we leave that precious little child all alone at Yolochka, my heart will break. Dr. Bohdan said he's healthy, and I believe him. The boy is afraid of us because we're strangers to him. It's a normal reaction. He's so vulnerable and tiny, he needs a family. I know he'll warm to us. We have to bring him home!"

"Agreed. I love you."

"Love you, too."

By the time we arrive back at the Svoboda hotel, the sun has set. The parking lot is dark and still. The ladies at the reception counter acknowledge us.

"*Dobryy vecher.* Good evening."

"Good evening." Albert's face is pensive.

We hike up to the fourth floor and my husband knocks on our adoption facilitator's guest room door.

"Hello, Sofia? It's Albert. Sandra is here with me, too. Can we please speak with you?" My husband's voice is slightly raised.

"Yes, absolutely. One minute, please."

I hear slow footsteps and the unlocking of a door latch. I watch the door open. The hopeful expression on Sofia's face tells me she's been expecting us.

"Ah! Yes, of course. Please, come in."

Despite my best efforts, I am unable to stop the flow of tears and intensity of feeling that engulf me. Albert does the talking for both of us while I nod my head in agreement, strangely unable to utter a single word. Sofia passes me tissues and holds my hand while I stand trembling between the two of them.

"Please, don't cry," Sofia implores me. "This is a moment to celebrate. Sandra, you and Albert have taken a very big decision. You will soon be the parents of a wonderful son!"

The Children's Home Director

Outside the hotel our chauffeur finishes a mobile phone call. He opens the back door of his sedan to let me in. Albert clambers in alongside me. Already seated to my right, Sofia moves closer to the window on her side. Iryna is riding shotgun.

The two ladies are once again professionally dressed and don full makeup; they are unmistakably serious about setting the proper tone with the Yolochka director. I'm confident my husband and I also convey an appropriate degree of respect in our corporate attire.

Yevgeny and Sofia trade a few words, and we're off.

Thankfully, the trip is quiet. Everyone is collecting their thoughts. Despite a night's sleep, I'm physically and mentally depleted. I want to make clear to the children's home director that we intend to adopt the boy we met. Hopefully, the man will agree to sign the necessary papers to move our file forward.

Stepping out of the car, my legs are wobbly, but I force myself to walk.

I carefully shut the main door of the children's home behind me so as not to irritate the front reception clerk. The administrator greets us with a slight wave of her wrinkly hand. She proudly shows off a long pink scarf draped around her shoulders and invites me to touch it. The matching hat appears to have a price tag still attached. The wool is cuddly soft. I smile at the woman, and she half-smiles back.

Two couples in the foyer are huddled together against the wall. They're conversing in Spanish with a man I assume is their facilitator or translator.

Sofia informs the administrator about our appointment. While the woman slowly punches in some numbers on the phone, we remove our coats and grab a chair.

Within minutes, I put my coat back around my shoulders, as the temperature in the foyer is chilly. The Spanish group remains standing against the wall; I wonder why they won't sit. Their consultant seems aggravated about something.

The quick snap of footsteps soon echoes from a nearby hallway. An olive-skinned man with shiny, jet-black hair and a dark fitted suit emerges from the left corridor. He clicks his heels together and makes a beeline for Sofia, vigorously shaking her hand. The two speak animatedly, as though they are friends. Sofia hands the gentleman a document and introduces him to Iryna. The two exchange brief pleasantries.

Sofia turns towards us. "Albert and Sandra, come. I am pleased to introduce you to Yaroslav Kyrylo Mazur, the director of Yolochka Children's Home."

The man extends a handshake to each of us. I grip his hand tightly and look him in the eyes, expressing the urgency of the matter we've come to address. He cranks his head to one side, grinning wryly at me.

Mazur's robust cologne wafts through the corridor as we follow him into his office. I'm surprised to see a working fireplace along the back wall. A couple of logs are crackling away; the office is much warmer than any other spaces I've seen in the building. I wonder if the fireplace is used regularly, or if it has been set alight for our benefit.

On the wooden mantelpiece are photographs of deer and woodcocks. A hunting rifle is mounted on the rack above.

A sumptuous woven rug with images of birds and other animals is placed in front of the hearth, along with a reclining chair and small side table. An ashtray on the table overflows with cigarette butts. I presume the director retreats to the hearth when he needs a break from his formal desk area.

Mazur motions for us to take a seat on a well-worn couch on one side of the room. The four of us manage to squeeze onto it.

The director rolls a chair out from behind his imposing desk, inching closer to the sofa and swiveling the seat to directly face my husband before sitting down. I notice the man's polished black shoes have wing tips.

Mazur runs his hand through his thick black mane and fixes his gaze on my husband.

"I understand you have an interest in one of the children in room S-11?"

Iryna is translating.

My husband's answer is swift. "Yes."

The director holds up the document Sofia gave him in the reception area.

"You have made the decision to adopt this child."

"Yes," Albert responds again, unequivocal.

Mazur puts the paper on his lap and reads it. A few moments later, he stands up and walks to the hearth, places the document down on the side table, and pulls out a cigarette from his jacket pocket.

Returning to the swivel chair, Mazur clicks a silver lighter, ignites the flame, and takes a long drag of the cigarette.

"Do you have the means to raise this child?"

"Yes, without question." Albert fixes his gaze on Mazur.

"What is the nature of your profession?"

"I run a commercial printing company in Toronto, Canada."

"You are the owner and proprietor?"

"Yes."

Mazur rises again, walks to the side table, flicks some ashes into the tray, and goes back to the swivel chair.

"Your wife will stay at home to raise the boy?"

"Of course, for a year at least, and then she may return to work, part-time or … we haven't made that decision yet. My wife works as a …"

"Are you aware of the boy's medical condition?"

What medical condition? Sofia pinches my arm just as I'm clearing my throat in preparation to speak. I stop myself.

"Umm … yes," Albert replies, appearing confused.

"Then it is your honest intention to make this child a part of your family, residing with you in your home in Canada?"

"Indeed."

"Do you understand that as a result of my granting permission, you will be required to apply to the regional court of Simferopol to adopt the child and will need to appear in front of a judge in a formal hearing to swear your lifelong commitment to and responsibility for this child?"

"Yes, we are aware."

As Mazur refuses to acknowledge my presence and Sofia implores me not to speak, I stay out of the conversation. I glance around the office. The window facing the front garden offers a view of rose bushes, tall spruce trees, children's swings, and climbing gear, but no one's outside.

The men stop talking. Mazur inhales a long puff of his smoke, gets up, and extinguishes his cigarette in the ashtray. He lifts our document, rolls the swivel chair back behind his desk, and takes a seat. There's a short back-and-forth conversation between Mazur and Sofia. Iryna doesn't translate; I assume they are discussing dry technical points.

Mazur retrieves a pen from his desk drawer and signs the bottom of the sheet of paper. He then stands up, walks toward my husband, and hands him the document.

"You will go to see the lawyer for Yolochka. I congratulate you and wish you well."

Albert rises from the couch and shakes hands with the director, who smiles politely and squeezes my husband's shoulder for emphasis. Albert's face conveys relief.

I pull myself up from the couch and extend my hand out, too, towards Mazur. He seems perturbed and responds with a half-hearted handshake, barely making eye contact. He raises his arm toward the door, indicating the meeting is over.

I ask about the condition of the children, how the home is doing, and what kind of aid the director may need to improve the life of its residents, but Iryna does not translate my questions, and Sofia's eyes widen as she cocks her head toward the door, making it clear the discussion is over. We're dismissed, and there's no point engaging the director any further.

It will take some getting used to, this hush-hush world of the Simferopol children's home, where everything is said and done under tight control and behind closed doors. Where are the children in all this? We haven't seen any, except for the child who will be our son. What obsession do Ukrainians have with men being the head of the family? Don't the bureaucrats realize that for most of the children being adopted, mothers will do the heavy lifting in raising them? Doesn't anyone want to know what women have to say?

Before traveling to Ukraine, I'd seen messages posted on internet chats about children living in Ukrainian children's homes who suddenly disappear, without a trace, in the middle of an adoption.

Our Toronto adoption agent, Laryssa Hrehoriv, acknowledged the rumours about a resurgent black market for children. She urged us to get the paperwork started as soon as we had made a decision to adopt a particular child because the existence of written documentation would improve the chances of safeguarding them from illegal activity. Iryna and Sofia confirmed they had no personal experience with such tragic situations, but concurred with Laryssa's belief that documentation was a form of insurance as we seek to complete the adoption.

Given Sofia's respected status as a representative of a charitable organization that supports Ukrainian children's homes, it's hard for me to believe we might find ourselves in the middle of any nasty business.

In the end, I'm glad I did not broach the subject of missing children with Mazur. It might have angered or offended him, and who knows what kind of impact that might have on our attempts to adopt a child from his facility? The boss doesn't project the air of a menacing or deceitful person, although I wasn't able to truly connect with him in a meaningful way.

On our way back to the reception area, Sofia verifies she'll coordinate a meeting with the lawyer as soon as possible. Before we leave Yolochka, one of the white-coated doctors greets my husband and I in the front lobby. She congratulates us on our decision to adopt the little boy.

Through Iryna's translation, the doctor explains the routine for daily visits with our son. As of now, we are allowed two-hour visits each morning and afternoon, aligned to the children's home schedule. We can take our boy outside for a walk in a stroller, weather permitting, or otherwise spend time indoors, although there is no designated area for parents to visit their children inside the home.

The physician says we can bring cookies for our son to snack on, but warns against providing any other food products, which are strictly forbidden. Is she joking? Cookies? For a malnourished child? I bite my lip, look at the woman and nod, signaling I understand the stipulations.

Once the doctor has left the reception area, Albert and I converse in Latvian that we'll ignore what the lady said about food restrictions because our son needs substantial nourishment.

Sofia looks pleased with how the morning has gone. "We will go to lunch now. I will ask Yevgeny to take us to Uzbek restaurant," she remarks, rubbing my back.

As we make our way to the front door, the Spanish consultant and a white-coated woman are in a heated conversation.

The two couples intently watch the banter, and they don't look happy.

"*Nyet.* No," the lady says.

"What's going on?" I ask.

"This is not our concern," Iryna responds, grimacing. "Please, let us go to the car."

******

"Son, it's our first outdoor picnic. We're going to have fun!" Albert is buoyant.

Our son—our *son*—is bundled up in a snowsuit as my husband pushes the stroller away from the children's home towards the woods. The buggy bobs up and down a small grassy hill. We've brought along a bottle of pear juice and cheese purchased from a green grocer for our child to snack on. We also have a bag of cookies to use as a ruse, should any caregivers from Yolochka surprise us on our journey.

"Do you think any of the white-coat people can see us here?" I ask my husband.

"No," he replies.

Like the previous day's visit, our son doesn't fuss as long as the carriage is moving. He's quietly enjoying the surrounding greenery.

"I'm going to try giving him some cheese," I say. "Hopefully he'll like it."

"Sure, we're completely out of sight of Yolochka now." Albert slows down the pace of the stroller to a crawl, then stops pushing.

He removes his backpack and puts it on the ground. I take the cheese bag and sipping cup out and put a small block of cheese in our son's hand.

"Here you go, little one." I'm smiling widely; can my boy sense the joy I feel in spending time with him?

The child looks at the cheese block. I take a piece of cheese, too, and show him I'm eating it. "See? Pop it into your mouth. Mmmm! Delicious!"

Our son puts the cheese in his mouth and eats it. I give him another piece. He takes that, and consumes it, too. Then another, and another.

"He likes it; I'm giving him more." Soon the cheese bag is empty.

"Ah! Ah!" he says.

"What about the juice?" Albert says.

I hold the sipping cup to help my son drink. Although the stroller isn't moving anymore, the child doesn't seem to mind. He finishes the juice, and I pour him more; he drinks a second cup.

My husband and I crouch down so our son can see us at his eye level while seated in the stroller. We smile and hold his hands and assure him, everything's fine, we're enjoying the day together. The child looks like he's about to cry. Albert quickly stands up, as do I, and my husband pushes the carriage forward. Crisis averted; the child's worried look disappears once the buggy is moving again.

At the entrance to the forest Albert stops the carriage. He waits for a moment to see if our boy might cry. When the child remains quiet, he lifts our son out and lets him stand on the ground. The child is motionless, holding on to the buggy. He looks ahead, into the forest, then turns his head slowly towards us.

I cheerily urge the boy: "Let's walk for a bit!"

I take my toddler's hand and motion for him to step forward with me. He remains standing in place. Soon the down-turned lip appears and the crying begins again.

"Forget it," Albert says. "He's wary of us and doesn't want to go into the forest. We can try walking together in a few days, once he's more accustomed to being with us."

I lift our boy and put him back in the stroller. The rest of the visit goes well. Our son is placid while Albert pushes the carriage back towards Yolochka. We do several laps of the children's home property.

Back at the anteroom to S-11, Albert and I hug and kiss our son and speak gently to him while waiting for a caregiver to arrive. He looks tired; we must have worn him out.

A young woman steps out from the interior living area. She moves her hands expressively while speaking, and takes the carriage from my husband. I slowly pass my son from my arms to hers; it's somehow less painful to release him back to the care of the children's home than to feel him being grabbed away from me. I try to remain composed while our child disappears behind a door.

How will I survive weeks of "visiting" my son? I want to take him home to Canada now!

******

Albert and I enjoy two days of outings where we repeatedly circle the Yolochka grounds with our little boy in a carriage. We tell our son a bit about us and why the three of us are spending time together. We sneak him food and walk a few steps together towards the edge of the forest. For our next outing, my husband and I have decided it's time to enter the forest.

It's a glorious, sunny day. Albert is pushing the stroller up and down the grassy hill leading to the woods. Our boy snacks along the way.

My husband rolls the buggy into the forest and finds a clearing. He stops the carriage and lifts our son out; the child seems less frightened now than on earlier visits.

The little fellow stands beside the stroller, staring tentatively at us. We let him take his time adjusting to the surroundings. I smile at him and nod my head to let the child know everything is good, there's no need to worry. Albert strokes our son's head.

The child cautiously observes the nearby trees and shrubs and is intrigued by the woodland clatter. Birds singing. Frogs yelping. Squirrels squeaking as they scamper along crackling tree trunks. Our boy turns his head, following the sounds and the animals making them. Sturdy pines and spruces surround us, emitting a sharp and sweet aroma, like freshly cut grass.

Our son takes a few small steps forward and stops.

"Yes," I tell him. "Let's explore together." I take my son's hand, encouraging him to keep walking. After a few steps, the child stops again. He looks up, eyes darting between mine and my husband's. Holding my hand, the boy toddles gingerly among decaying twigs, moss-covered branches, rustling leaves, and small stones dotting the moist earth.

Has he ever been allowed to walk in these woods before?

My son lets go of my hand. He runs his fingers slowly across fallen branches near his feet, picks up small twigs and smacks them together. Albert and I watch as he pulls a damp stick close to his face, and licks it.

My husband shows our child how to cross two sticks forming an "X", and to draw patterns in the air. I'm incredibly content to watch them. A while later, I join the fun. Seated on the ground across from our little boy, I push a pile of decomposing leaves around with a twig. Soon, he does the same.

We remain in the forest all afternoon, getting more acquainted with one another. We share some mint tea I've brought along in a thermos. I make sure it's not too hot before letting our son try it. He seems more comfortable with us, allowing me to lift him up, tickle his nose, and rub it against my own.

When it's time to leave, Albert helps our son back into the carriage and pushes the stroller as it weaves its way back to the children's home, looking like he wished he never had to let go.

Wall of Rain

It's raining hard in Simferopol. A torrent of water pounds the trees and parking lot of our hotel. The sky is dark. Our third-floor balcony is soaked; wind relentlessly whips water onto it. The surrounding pines and cedars bend submissively from the force of the storm. An appropriate act of God, I'm thinking, as the downpour aptly reflects my state of mind.

I should celebrate that my husband and I have permission from the children's home director to pursue our son's adoption. I'm enormously happy and relieved. At the same time, Albert and I won't have unconstrained access to our child until more administrative tasks are completed, a judge has decreed the adoption to be legal, and numerous documents are authorized, stamped, and notarized.

According to the materials our Toronto adoption agent, Laryssa, shared about children residing in institutional settings, I have to acknowledge that our child needs time to adjust to my husband and I as parents, to learn a new language and culture, and to understand and accept that his whole world is changing. And, while I believe the adoption will transform his life for the better, he'll also need to grieve, and recover from, what he's leaving behind.

I retrieve the adoption three-ring binder from my carry-on bag and read through some of the posts Laryssa provided about children living in post-Soviet institutions. I want to understand what our little boy may be grappling with, and figure out how best to help.

Several clinicians point to children in these settings having multiple caregivers who cannot devote much time to an individual child because of scarce resources. Rooms where children live lack stimulating developmental toys or playthings. Some children are malnourished because inadequate food supplies are eaten by the caregivers, who are undernourished themselves. A number of children are physically, psychologically or sexually abused and can be exposed to dangerous environmental hazards.

How to know what goes on at Yolochka outside of visiting hours?

Further in the posts, the tone becomes more positive and aligns with some of what Dr. Bohdan said about the state of Ukrainian children's homes. Conditions have improved since 1989, when the formerly occupied countries of Eastern Europe became aware of new and alternative ways to care for institutionalized children. Funding care remains very challenging, but there is now an eagerness to learn on both sides. Western educators and clinicians may have more financial resources than do their Eastern European counterparts, but much can be learned about what has been going on in institutional settings, and what is or isn't working. When parents from Western countries bring their newly adopted children home, the help they and their child need may not be clearly understood, articulated or available. However, now that the iron curtain has lifted, more dialogue should flow.

I wonder what my son is doing at this very moment. To be sure, he's under the strict control of the ladies who oversee their charges. Is he warm enough in the storm? Does he have enough to eat? Is anyone telling him he's loved? I don't know.

The email we sent home to our family about the boy was brief: "We met him, he is absolutely wonderful and shy, and we want to raise him! We're confident he'll soon become our son."

The four hours a day Yolochka has granted us to spend with our boy while we complete the Crimea adoption procedures will allow us to sneak him nutritious food, help his mind and body develop, and shower him with love. It's understandable the child needs time to adjust to the two new adults in his life; I get it. We can't just show up, pick him up, and leave.

Still, in my heart I feel cheated. I want the freedom to be with my son twenty-four hours a day. I need to physically hold him, soothe him, and take him anywhere I choose, whenever I want, because in order to thrive, he needs the ongoing support of a caring family.

Most of all, my heart aches to make up for all the time my boy has lived without a mother's love.

I'm determined to give my son the best opportunities that life in Canada can afford him. The adoption posts Laryssa shared contain a number of references to internationally adopted children having "special needs." This type of labelling causes me to grit my teeth. Any child may encounter difficulties throughout their life. These can be addressed through multiple potential approaches and solutions. I believe it's best to leave the decisions on what type of care may be required, with the child and parents themselves.

As a mama bear, I will fiercely protect and advocate for my cub and will teach him to speak out about what he really needs in order to thrive.

In the Svoboda dining room at breakfast, we learn from our translator, Iryna, that there will be no visit to Yolochka this morning due to an unforeseen "situation." We're told the matter is not related to our son, nor to John and Mary's kids, but the end result is that no one is allowed to enter the grounds.

Yevgeny agrees to drive my husband and I to a grocer as we want to pick up some food supplies. We borrow a huge umbrella from the front desk clerks, put on our boots and coats, and head out in the storm.

We're back at the hotel within an hour. I fill our small fridge with the purchases and prepare a bag with dirty laundry. The hotel staff promises everything will be cleaned and pressed within twenty-four hours.

Apart from the hotel laundry service I'm grateful to be relieved of everyday tasks—preparing meals, tidying up, and cleaning our living space—which are being handled by the Svoboda staff. The adoption demands have rendered me incapable of managing most daily chores.

I'm singularly focused on expressing love to our son, helping him flourish, and completing the adoption paperwork so we can all leave Yolochka together as soon as possible. Nothing else is of consequence.

With the unexpected free time this morning, my husband plants himself on a chair in our guest room to continue reading his Martin Luther historical novel. I lie down for a nap.

A while later, the phone rings. Albert answers the call and soon hangs up.

"Iryna's invited us to join her at the Uzbek restaurant for lunch. We can visit our son at the children's home afterwards."

I'm beaming. "What a relief, that's wonderful!"

******

The heavy rain continues; we're advised by the children's home staff to spend our afternoon time with our son indoors.

The brown wooden entrance door to the S-11 living space creaks open. Our child is handed to me. He's petite and adorable in a bright teal, red, and purple Mickey Mouse sweatshirt and matching teal and purple checkered pants. I forgot again how light he feels in my arms.

He gazes inquiringly at us. "What are you two doing here again?" his face is saying.

As there's no designated space for adoptive parents to conduct an indoor visit, the three of us must walk the halls of Yoluchka.

We move along the dim hallways on the main floor. There is an orderly line of a dozen or so couples snaking up and down the corridors with their children. It warms my heart to see the kids bring the bleak building to life, even though most of the youngsters are quiet and subdued; many are so frail they must be carried by their parents.

These are the beginning days of families being formed and new languages being learned. I conjecture that the children are seriously perplexed about what is going on. Why all of a sudden two unfamiliar grownups are spending so much time with them. Do they have an inkling that the adults have chosen to parent them, to protect, support, and love them for the rest of their lives?

The parents we pass in the halls are obviously not native to the area. None of their conversations resemble Ukrainian or Russian, as far as I can tell. The grownups are speaking tenderly with their kids in English, Spanish, and German. I suppose local people choose to adopt much younger girls and boys who are living in some other children's homes because they have the legal right to do so.

Albert and I take turns carrying our son; he doesn't protest. We use the time to tell him about the extended family eagerly waiting to meet him in Canada, the United States and Latvia. We describe his three older sisters, aged twelve, seventeen, and nineteen, his grandparents, aunts, uncles, and cousins, and the gray and white kitty who will surely be a loyal companion at home.

Holding our little boy palpably soothes him. I say "hello" to the parents in the corridor who are willing to make eye contact, and hope for future opportunities to engage with them.

As we can't feed our son anything other than cookies while inside the building, my husband retrieves a bag of sweets we've brought along in his backpack. My little boy readily consumes them while the white-coated staffers stride by. The women nod approvingly. Our son holds as many cookies as he can manage in each hand and keeps eating until they're gone. He stretches out his hands to ask for more. We eagerly indulge him.

At the end of the visit, Albert puts our boy down to stand in the hallway. We each take one of his hands and slowly walk him back to the room where he resides. We wait for a few moments in the anteroom until a caregiver appears.

Natasha receives our son from my husband's arms and says, "*Spasibo*," which I take to mean "Thank you."

"*Spasibo*," I say back to her, and she shuts the door. "Goodbye, my little prince," I mournfully declare in a near whisper.

Albert and I head down the dark halls again to the Yolochka front entrance. My heart is wounded.

"You realize this is our new routine," I tell my husband. "A rational person would readily accept the rules and regulations of the children's home, the legal requisites, and the time we'll have to devote in Crimea to let our son get used to us. I must be completely irrational, because the three or more remaining weeks of visits and adoption bureaucracy yet to come seem like a very long time to me. Our son needs us *now*, not in three weeks. He's already family, he's in my heart. I feel it every minute of every day."

"I hear you," my husband responds, tipping his head to one side. "I would love to head home now, too, with our sweet little boy. I can't wait for the girls to meet him. It's awful leaving him every day, but we have to respect the rules and take it one day at a time."

Week Three

The Backpack

Sofia is sitting on a couch in the Svoboda hotel lobby, writing in her leather notebook. My husband and I jog past her on our way out the main door for breakfast, as we only have half an hour before we need to leave for the children's home. Albert and I have decided to show the wait staff with our hands what we'd like to eat if none of our Russian-speaking companions can be found in the dining hall.

The large eatery is quiet. A server arrives at our table and pours tea. Albert flips one hand down on top of the other, indicating he'd like to order eggs over easy. The woman appears to understand and nods her head. I repeat the same hand signals.

A short time later, the server returns. She positions a plate of eggs over easy in front of me. There's also a slice of whole grain toast and a small pot of peach jam. My husband receives

the same. We attack the meal; it tastes like home. I suggest to Albert that the only thing missing is a strong cup of coffee.

"I'd actually kill for that," he replies, deadpan.

Leaving the dining hall, I see Yevgeny smoking a cigarette outside the Svoboda main entrance. Sofia is in the front seat of the chauffeur's vehicle on her cell phone. Albert and I scramble into the rear. When the facilitator finishes her call, she turns and looks back to tell us she's been trying to get us a meeting with the children's home lawyer. It's taking a bit longer than anticipated, but Sofia is confident an appointment can soon be arranged.

Meanwhile, I'm thrilled to have more time to spend with our son.

"We go to Yolochka now," Sofia affirms, signalling for the driver to leave. Yevgeny hits the gas.

When the car pulls up to the children's home, Sofia lets us know the chauffeur will retrieve us after the morning visit. She is continuing on to another location and we will see her later in the day.

At Yolochka, the sun is out. It's not too brisk and the sky is brilliant blue. The black-and-white cats lounge by the front entrance. One is curled up sleeping with paws tucked under his stomach, another stands tall inspecting us, and the third grooms herself with her tongue. The standing kitty meows as we pass her.

"Good morning to you, too!" I tell the cat.

Inside the foyer, the elderly administrator notes our arrival and nods us through.

Our son is fully dressed in a snowsuit, boots, and hat, ready to go outside, when we arrive at the anteroom of S-11.

A dark-haired woman lifts him off the top of the cubbyhole shelf and hands him to me.

"*Spasibo!*" I say, cuddling my child. The caregiver responds with some words in Russian. I kiss our son and tell him in Latvian that Albert and I are so happy to see him again. He gazes calmly at me, then turns his head to acknowledge my husband.

Albert carries the stroller down the stairs to the outdoors while I descend with our child in my arms. Our son allows my husband to strap him into the carriage without any fuss.

We're off toward the back of the Yolochka grounds and beyond. Up and down the small hill, Albert pushes the stroller. We stop briefly so I can pull out the bag of cheese from his backpack. Our son watches intently as I hand him small blocks to eat along the way.

Deep in the forest, we park the buggy. I retrieve the sipping cup with juice from the backpack and hand it to my boy. He brings it to his mouth and empties it. My husband lifts out a small yoghurt container I take it, open it, and show our son a spoon. I scoop out some yoghurt with the spoon and feed it to him. He eagerly swallows the yoghurt. I motion for him to scoop out more with the spoon himself. He takes the spoon, shakes it, and smiles.

"Yes," I say, smiling back, "the spoon goes into the packet, and you lift the yoghurt out."

I bring the container closer to my son's hand. He looks inside, scoops out the yoghurt, puts it into his mouth, and swallows.

"Ooorh!" he babbles with delight. He devours the remaining yoghurt. I clean his face and the front of his jacket with a disposable towelette and put the dining accessories away in a plastic bag. Albert comments that we'll need to bring at least two yoghurt containers for the next visit.

Our little boy is eager to be let out of the stroller. Once freed, he takes a moment to scan the surroundings. I watch him meander off searching for small twigs and branches, collect a few sticks one by one, throw them to the ground, and smack some against a tree.

"Ooorh!"

My husband joins the fun. The two of them play with sticks and branches and sweep their hands through the verdant underbrush.

"Son, these giant trees are strong and handsome; they're green all year," Albert schools our boy. "They help keep the air clean. The forest smells wonderful because of everything nature brings together here."

"Dhizz!" our child responds.

I love the sound of his voice.

Albert suggests a game of hide-and-go seek. He hides behind a nearby tree. "Come and find me!" he calls.

"Let's go!" I take my son's hand. Bit by bit, we walk over to the tree. "Papa, we caught you!" I tap Albert on the arm.

My husband runs behind another tree.

"Come on, where did Daddy go?" I ask.

Our son grasps the point of the game. As Albert moves deeper into the forest, hiding behind more trees, the boy holds my hand tight and we walk to find him.

"Ooorh!"

"Okay, now you two hide and I'll look for you," my husband proposes.

We duck behind a dense conifer. Albert counts to ten and comes looking for us.

"Ready or not, here I come!"

When my husband spots us, I laugh and our boy squeals. I feel alive and free and full of love for our son.

When everyone is tired, we plop down on the ground, cross-legged, and Albert sings a Latvian folk song about a baby goat. Our boy's eyes widen. He stares at my husband as if the sound coming from his mouth is sacred. When the singing stops, our son wants more. He points to my husband and says, "Meh! Meh!"

Albert sings another Latvian folk song about a rooster in the early morning. I join my husband in harmony. Our son is spellbound.

"Come on, we have to get back now," Albert declares, standing up after the song ends. He points to his wristwatch.

"Hmmm. This lovely morning together has to be interrupted up by the children's home schedule," I quip.

"Stop complaining. We're coming back after lunch; let's make the best of it."

******

After a quick bowl of soup at the Uzbek restaurant, Yevgeny drives us back to the Svoboda hotel for a short rest before the afternoon visit with our son.

With nothing else to do, I flip through the pages of my adoption binder. The posts from Laryssa's emails about adopting institutionalized children are starting to get well worn.

One topic discussed is how the adjustment to family life for an internationally adopted child will not happen overnight.

It will unfold over time through many interactions between parents and child, and, in our case, also through relations with three older sisters, along with aunts, uncles, cousins, and grandparents. Everyone in the family will need to adapt and learn. Agreed.

However, the biggest demands for change will be placed on our son. The shift to family life will require him to completely relearn how to live. Everything he knows now will be replaced by a new language, social customs, geography and culture. Every interaction and routine will change. All of the people around him will be different. From the food he eats to the attention he receives, the colours, textures, sights, smells and sounds around him, everything will be new.

A child cannot be expected to easily master such complicated scenarios on their own. The addition of a new toddler to our blossoming blended family will challenge all of us to create more space in our hearts. Undoubtedly, we will trip and fall along the way, and that will be part of the joy of the journey.

Albert tugs at my arm. "Put your papers away now, it's time to leave."

I snap the binder shut. We make our way down to the lobby and out the hotel front door.

We're back at Yolochka for the afternoon visit. All is quiet. Natasha emerges from the children's quarters with our son to prepare him for the outdoors. He seems sleepy, rubbing his eyes like he's just woken up.

I use hand signals to let the caregiver know I can dress him; my child doesn't seem to mind as I get him ready to go.

Albert smiles adoringly as he steps closer to our son. "Hey, my boy, let's go for another walk outside." He gently touches our toddler's arm. "It will be fun, I promise."

Our son sees that my husband is wearing the backpack. He perks up.

"Ah! Ah!"

Albert pulls the backpack tighter on his back, moving it out of the child's sight for now. We don't want to give the caregivers any clues about what's in the bag.

With our son dressed and ready to go, Natasha returns to the children's living space.

My husband hurriedly pushes the carriage away from the Yolochka grounds. Our child keeps turning his head around, looking to see where the backpack is. Albert stops the stroller when we're clearly out of sight. I retrieve the cheese bag from the backpack.

"Ah! Ah!" our boy exclaims, taking pieces of cheese from my hand and eating them all the way to the forest.

Out of the stroller, our son observes my husband placing the backpack on the ground and removing and opening two containers of yoghurt. "Ah! Ah!"

I hand my child the spoon. He takes one of the yoghurt containers, empties it, then the other, and downs the pear juice in the sipping cup.

Happy to be fed, our boy stands quietly for a moment. He listens intently to the humming insects, birdsongs, and animals rustling nearby.

"Meh! Meh!"

"Yes, we love being in the woods. It's peaceful and calm here," Albert states.

Our toddler is off to study the ground cover, turning over pinecones and sticks, pushing pieces of crumbling bark around with his tiny fingers, and collecting a few pebbles. He brings the small stones over to me. I put out my hand; he drops them in my palm.

"Ooorh!"

The three of us stomp through the damp earth under our feet, crushing decomposing stumps, decaying branches, and fallen leaves.

Back at the clearing where we left the carriage, we all lie down, face up. The sky is sapphire blue. Tops of soaring conifers are swaying slightly as a gentle breeze moves through them. I feel hope and contentment in our private forest world.

"Do you think it's a good idea to lie here?" I query. "We're all getting wet and dirty."

"Dhizz!"

"I could stay like this for a while," Albert confesses. "It's hard to express how much I love the woods. Through all my years of Boy Scout trips, I cherished every minute I could spend outside, in nature. I want to remember these special first days together—the three of us—in this beautiful forest. Our son will be grown before we know it, and we won't be stomping around or lying down in the woods together anymore."

"Meh! Meh!"

Albert and I both burst out laughing.

"Yes, son, it's true," my husband retorts. "We'll snap our fingers and you'll be a man, and then you can explain to us what 'meh, meh' means."

The Secret Room

My husband and I have an hour's free time before leaving for a morning visit with our son at the children's home. I sort and put away our clothes into the hotel room wardrobe and pull out the adoption binder from my carry-on bag. While Albert has finished his Martin Luther book and is now reading *Cold Mountain*, I'm behind on reviewing the materials that Laryssa, our Toronto adoption agent, provided.

Having met our son and spent time with him, he seems absolutely perfect. Being with him feels normal and easy. He enjoys playing in the forest with us, I'm sure of it. He now readily expresses joy and is trying to speak. I realize it's early days for the three of us, but I want to believe that whatever will happen in the future, we'll face it confidently together as a family.

It's a bit nuts, I suppose, that Albert and I only speak Latvian to the boy, but we don't have much choice. Neither of us can converse in Russian, and in Canada, our whole extended family speaks Latvian at home. I have faith our son will quickly learn to understand what we're saying to him and, eventually, be able to respond back in Latvian. He can learn English in school. We'll also try to teach him about Ukraine, and I hope he shows some interest in learning about the country and its rich culture.

I scan more of the posts Laryssa shared that were prepared by researchers for members of the Adoption from Ukraine Internet Club.

There's a post about the challenges children encounter when they have been transported from one culture into another. Some internationally adopted children may have difficulty processing and responding to information or be overly sensitive to things in their environment. A child who has lived through separation and loss could experience depression. If a child has been subjected to abuse or neglect, they could suffer some degree of trauma and stress disorder.

There are several "disorders" described in the materials that a formerly institutionalized child could suffer from, but given that every child is unique and some children are inevitably more resilient than others, only time will tell what our family will be presented with. Every relationship we as humans enter into is a risk. Adopting our beautiful son is a risk I must take.

I'm relieved when Albert tells me to put away the binder and get ready to leave for the children's home. My head is spinning.

******

I'm surprised to see that the door to the secret interior room where our son resides has been left wide open. My husband and I are eager for the morning visit. A caregiver standing about a meter back from the door waves us inside.

Our boy spots us from the back of the room and stands up. A caregiver takes his hand and walks him over to us. The woman says a few words, and our son raises his arms. Albert lifts the little fellow up and cradles him on his elbow.

The lady is not a caregiver we've previously seen, but she obviously knows the children and is aware of which child we're coming to visit. She hands me a piece of paper with a handwritten message in Cyrillic. The number twelve is the only thing I can understand. I assume it might refer to the number of children dwelling in the room.

The caregiver extends her arm and gestures with a sweeping motion that we can take a look around. The main living area of the room is sparse but sizeable. Sheer curtains line a wall of windows, allowing plenty of sunlight to enter. The linoleum floor is well-worn but clean. A bathroom directly behind the living room has a sunken tub. Adjacent sleeping quarters have rows of small wooden cots; I count twelve in total.

The caregiver taps her hand on the railing of one of the beds; I assume that's the one our son sleeps in.

We return to the main living area. Small children are sitting, crawling, or waddling around, silently for the most part. One boy aggressively rocks back and forth on a hobbyhorse. Another repeatedly bangs his own head against a playpen railing. There aren't any toys to play with or books to enjoy that the children could reach, but there are playthings tacked high up on a wall. Two women direct the activity in the room, but they don't seem to be engaging much with their charges.

Some of the children are more alert than their counterparts, displaying curiosity about what is happening around them. Others stare impassively at nothing. There is little interaction among the children. None of the boys or girls respond when I smile at them or greet them, except for our son, which I realize is actually healthy behaviour, given that children are rightly wary of strangers.

It's hard to know what to think after seeing the children's room; most of the girls and boys just seem so sad. I reflect on Dr. Bohdan's comments about children waiting for future parents who may never come to bring them home. It knocks the stuffing out of me.

Albert motions to the caregivers that we'll be taking our son outdoors for the morning visit. A lady nods. We quickly dress the boy in the anteroom, and leave.

I'm dispirited as we dart away from the building with the stroller bouncing up and down. Having finally seen the secret room where children wander aimlessly and appear to be cut adrift, I want to know more about my son's daily routine. What types of early childhood development activities might be happening and how are they carried out? I make a mental note to ask Iryna to assist so she can translate for us.

Approaching the forest, our son keeps turning his head around in the carriage, looking back at my husband to see where the backpack is. He screeches loudly when Albert stops momentarily, removes the backpack and places it on the ground.

"Ah! Ah!" He points to the backpack.

Albert helps our son out of the stroller. The child heads straight for the backpack, fiddles for a moment until he figures out how to undo the clasp, then triumphantly opens the pack and pulls out the bag of cheese. He carries the cheese bag as he proudly walks the rest of the way into the forest, munching his food.

******

Iryna is sipping clear broth at the Uzbek restaurant when Albert and I arrive to meet her for lunch. A server takes our order.

"Can we please have one meatball soup and one borscht?" Albert says.

The steaming hot soup is set down in front of us in a few short minutes. We get right to it. In between sips, I ask Iryna if she might have time to return to Yolochka with us in the afternoon so we can become more familiar with our child's living conditions and daily routines.

"Of course," Iryna responds, smiling. "I have no pressing appointments this afternoon; your timing is good. I will confirm with the children's home before we depart."

Iryna's cheerful response brightens my day.

For dessert, I gulp down an instant coffee with milk, then order another.

"You sure about that?" my husband asks.

"Absolutely. I need caffeine to stimulate my brain so I can ask the caregivers the right questions."

Back at Yolochka, in the room where my son lives, the mood is quiet and most of the children are now out of sight. I spot our tiny boy crouched near a wall, moving small slippers around and stacking them. When he sees my husband and I approach, he drops the slippers and raises his arms up towards me. I pick our son up; he rests his head against my chest.

"Hi, sweetie," I say. I feel his body relax. "Daddy and I are going to speak to the ladies for a bit."

Iryna motions for us to follow her to the other side of the room. She introduces a short, rosy-cheeked caregiver who has agreed to share information about the children's daily meals and routine, with Iryna translating. I pass my son to my husband, as I want to write the information down.

"Hello, my boy," Albert says, smiling.

The dark-haired woman extends her small hand to me. Her handshake is limp.

"The children are well looked after," she assures us, in a high-pitched voice. "Regarding nutritional needs, please be aware that we provide the residents with milk porridges, cottage cheese, and other dairy foods such as boiled eggs. They also receive mashed potatoes, soups, fruit compotes, cookies, bread rolls, and tea."

I'm writing in my notebook as fast as I can, but the lady is speaking quickly.

I see my boy's eyes dart back and forth between the caregiver, Iryna, my husband, and I. He's curious about what's happening and trying to follow the conversation. What a difference from the first time we met. It's wonderful to see our boy progress and to know he's getting more and more comfortable with his mom and dad.

The caregiver outlines the daily routine.

"The children are roused at 7:00. Breakfast is at 8:00, and classes or games follow. Lunch is at noon, then it's nap time, snacks at 15:30, with more classes or games after that. Dinner is at 18:30, and at 20:00, they are offered an evening snack. Then bedtime."

I hurry to scribble down the times and activities, and ask the caregiver to describe the classes and games.

"All of the children participate in regular learning." She is finally slowing down the pace of her words. "There is a music lesson twice a week; speech, daily for fifteen minutes with caregivers; and once a week each child has an individual session with a speech pathologist. In addition, physical development periods and sensory development classes to distinguish forms, shapes, colours, and sizes are provided."

I'm heartened by the developmental activities described, the one-on-one speech lessons, and the breadth of nutritional foods being offered to the children. But I'm wondering about the formality of it all. Do any of these activities include hugs, joking around, or high-fives? Is this type of question even culturally appropriate to ask? Do I need to slap myself for being too North American in my world view?

There is a short back-and-forth verbal exchange between the caregiver and Iryna before the woman politely excuses herself.

Iryna looks at me awkwardly and says, "The caregiver would like to inform you that any introduction of new food products needs to be provided in small portions, that is, one teaspoon at a time, no more."

"Understood."

Albert and I trade sheepish glances. We dress our son, and quickly head outdoors.

With only an hour left before the afternoon visit ends, we race to the forest, our son in a carriage. The toddler is eager to see what's in the backpack. Pointing to the straps on my husband's shoulders, he confidently exclaims:

"Ah! Ah!"

Out of view of the children's home, Albert stops and releases the stroller clip, and removes his backpack, placing it on the ground. Our little boy climbs out of the carriage, pops the latch on the backpack and pulls out his snack.

"Ah! Ah!" His cheeks are packed with cheese.

"Careful, don't speak with your mouth full," I sweetly tell him.

In the forest, our son closely follows and mimics what my husband is doing: running his hands along the brittle bark of a mature spruce; putting his face against a tree to smell it; squishing pine needles between his thumbs and fingers; and making buzzing sounds, like insects.

"Bzzzz! Bzzzz! Bzzzz!"

The three of us sit, cross-legged, on the ground. We slap sticks and branches together, trying to see which ones break easily and which ones make the loudest noise. After a time, my husband sings the folk song about the baby goat that he sang on the previous visit. Our son drops the sticks and smiles at Albert elatedly.

"Meh! Meh!"

My husband and I sing the rooster in the morning song in harmony; our son's mouth falls wide open.

When we stop singing, our child stands up. He smiles, points at us and yells, "Dhizz!"

"Oh my!" I say. "Shall we play hide and seek?"

******

I am allowed to remain in the living space of my son's room at the children's home to observe the feeding and bathing at lunch time. For reasons unknown, my husband is asked to remain in the front reception area.

A stack of small bowls, spoons, and plastic bibs have been placed on a round table surrounded by toddler-size chairs. I'm curious to see what the children's lunch will consist of, as a pleasing bouquet of garlic and cabbage has wafted into the room.

My son is carried to the table by a caregiver. She seats him on a small chair and places a plastic bib around his neck; he instantly becomes agitated. I count two thin slices of carrot, a bit of cabbage and one small piece of potato in his soup bowl. The feeding is done in less than a minute, with four spoons of broth entering my son's mouth before he is ripped away from the bowl, screaming.

The caregiver hands my crying son to me, and says something in Russian, devoid of expression. I'm guessing she's telling me, "Please, take him; there are many more to feed."

I watch in disbelief as my child is still visibly hungry but not given any more. One by one, the remaining girls and boys are brought to the table to each receive their tiny portions, as well. The cries of hunger go unanswered; I have to admit, the caregiver is simply doing her job.

I try to comfort my son, carrying him around the room in my arms, but he is inconsolable. After all the kids have received their miniscule rations, the caregivers prepare a circle of plastic potties on the floor in the centre of the cold room for the children to sit on.

The caregiver motions for me to give her my son. Reluctantly, I hand him over. Each child, including my boy, is positioned on a pot. Not a single boy or girl in the group makes a fuss.

The children remain motionless until the entire group has finished their business and the caregivers allow the kids to stand up. I check my wristwatch; the silent potty session (and waiting for permission to move) has lasted thirty-four minutes. I can't recall a similar situation in Canada where I've seen children between the ages of one to three remain immobile, not moving for that amount of time, for any reason other than to sleep. Are they so resigned to their circumstances that they know resistance is futile?

It's now apparent that my son is not wearing diapers while in his living space. During our visits, he's been readied with a diaper. It occurs to me the caregivers have figured out we are feeding our son more than just cookies during our visits as his diaper is likely full when we return him to the home.

The woman signals for me to follow her to the adjoining washroom where my boy will be cleaned after potty time.

She strips the child naked and makes him stand straight up in the bathtub without moving. My boy keeps his hands straight down by his sides, and the caregiver sprays his body with freezing cold water, front and back, with a vigorous shower head. The child's face turns purple from crying.

My son is handed back to me to dry off and dress. I'm given a clean diaper, but the caregiver makes sure I understand the diaper bag is running out and it's up to my husband and I to provide more.

"*Paam-pehrs*," she says.

"*Da*." I got it. The photo on the bag shows disposable diapers.

I wrap my shivering child in a towel and dress him. While he's strangely quiet now, my son looks intently at me in a way that tells me unequivocally he's miserable.

"I know you're sad, I see it. But we'll all be together soon. Daddy and I will bring you home and we'll take very good care of you. We love you. The ladies here are doing the best they can."

I pull my son close and hug him tight. "I promise, it won't be much longer."

While forcing a smile to comfort my child, inside I'm distressed and anxious. How long can this ridiculous dance go on? Why can't we openly give our son all the nutritious food he needs *now*, and the loving care he rightly deserves?

My brain is telling me to leave the children's home with my son. I hurriedly carry him to the front lobby. When we reach my husband, tears flow.

"Let's get out of here," I say.

We go outside and head toward the front playscape area.

"What's wrong?", Albert asks. "Do you want a granola bar? We won't have time to go out for lunch."

"No, I don't want anything; I'm sick to my stomach. We need to get away from here with our son and never come back."

We walk to the far side of the playscape at the front of the building that is mostly out of view of the Yolochka staff. We sneak our son his snack. If any of the workers dare approach to challenge us about the food we've brought, I resolve to physically take them down.

Albert helps our frail child climb a wooden ramp on the playscape. The boy carefully holds on while my husband demonstrates how to get up and down the slide and how to jump off a hefty wooden stump.

It occurs to me why I'd been invited to observe the mealtime, apart from getting the message about needing to provide diapers to the children's home. The caregivers want my husband and I to know the children are underfed, although it wasn't news to me.

Later in the day I ask Sofia how we could help the children at Yolochka meet their nutritional needs. In her sweet way, she suggests we go to a market, purchase some food, and discreetly leave it with the kitchen staff.

"Whatever you can provide will be appreciated."

******

At an open-air Simferopol market, hundreds of ragtag stalls overflow with fresh vegetables and fruit, housewares, clothing, and electronics. With help from Yevgeny, we buy a crate of apples, a ten-kilogram bag of carrots, numerous heads of cabbage, and a huge sack of potatoes. We also purchase cookies, blocks of cheese, yoghurt, and juice to give to our son. We'd hoped to find some bread, cucumbers, meat or fish, but are unsuccessful.

Diapers, also, are nowhere in sight. As our chauffeur speaks no English, we enlighten him with hand signals as to what we we're looking for. The driver laughs when he realizes what we need and escorts us to the appropriate stall.

My husband has brought along a piece of paper to the market. He's traced the outline of our son's foot, so that we can buy him warm winter boots.

Yevgeny directs us to a children's footwear vendor. We choose a pair of boots that are one or two sizes bigger than our son's traced foot, as we're certain he'll quickly grow into them. The leather is sturdy and the boots are well insulated.

"*Türkiye*," Yevgeny says, giving a thumbs up. We understand this to mean the boots are made with Turkish leather.

Back at the hotel, we cube some cheese and prepare for our next visit to the children's home.

Yevgeny enters the Yolochka reception area together with Albert and I; each of us carry some of the food purchased at the market. The driver explains to the front desk administrator that we would like to donate the food to the kitchen.

The elderly lady nods her approval, and we follow Yevgeny down several hallways to the kitchen entrance, which is located in a back area on the ground floor of the building. Our driver knocks on an opaque glass window. A lady in a hairnet slides the window open. The two briefly converse, and the window closes. Yevgeny points for us to leave the food bags and apple crate in front of a nearby door. He knocks on the door. The woman in the hairnet opens it, looks at the food products, smiles appreciatively, and heads back inside.

Marching back to the front lobby through the warren of dark hallways after the visit with our son, I wonder why the children's home doesn't formally require all adoptive parents to provide a donation of food or money to supplement the nutritional requirements of its residents. Is this an issue of national pride that the question cannot be openly raised, are there concerns about the safety or quality of food being brought in, or does asking for food donations or money infer some form of bribery?

"If I was in charge at Yolochka, things would be run differently," I tell my husband on the ride back to the Svoboda hotel.

"Yes, undeniably," he retorts, incredulous. "It's easy to criticize, but we really don't have any idea what the children's home staff are dealing with. Laying blame on people who scramble every day to keep children alive and well on a shoestring budget is unfair."

Of course, Albert is right. I need to stop thinking about what seems wrong or uncomfortable from my Canadian lens, and put all of my energy toward successfully completing the Ukraine adoption so we can bring our boy home.

The Lawyer

My husband lifts a plush teddy bear out from his suitcase that he's brought with him from Canada to give our son. His eyes light up.

"I want to bring the bear with us today."

"Great idea!" I respond.

"But we won't leave the teddy at Yolochka," he adds. "I mean, they don't exactly let the kids play with anything. They'll probably tack it up on the wall if we leave it for him."

"Bring it anyway. Our son can play with it when we visit. When we pick him up to take him home to Canada, he'll have the teddy bear for company on the trip."

Albert stuffs the bear into his backpack. I add a bag of cut-up cheese, a bottle of juice, the sipping cup, some crackers, and two bananas.

There's a knock at the door.

"Yes?" my husband calls out.

"Hello, Albert and Sandra. It is me, Sofia."

Albert fights with the key and opens the door.

"Hi. Are we late? We're just getting ready to come downstairs …"

"No, no. Take your time, but ... you won't be going to Yolochka today."

"Pardon me, Sofia, what are you saying?" My husband sounds miffed.

"Documents need to be processed," Sofia responds. "Both of you must accompany us to lawyer's office in Simferopol."

I sigh. Sofia's business suit and teased hair indicate the adoption formalities continue to demand our attention.

I wonder what our boy will be thinking when we don't show up to visit him. Will he worry that we're never coming back? The three of us have grown close, and we're making progress as a family.

Sofia steps into our room for a moment. She reminds us the children's home director has done his bit, but the lawyer is another story entirely. To move the adoption through administrative channels in Crimea, we need the lawyer representing the home to give us an official, stamped declaration that from Yolochka's point of view, and not only the director's, we're cleared to adopt our son.

After numerous phone calls to the lawyer's office, Sofia has finally secured an appointment; it's for today.

"Let's not empty the backpack," I tell my husband. "Maybe we'll get to see our boy at the end of the day."

Albert's eyes are downcast; I can tell he's sad we'll miss a morning visit with our son, and so am I. He slaps his cap on his head and jangles and jingles the room key until the guest room is locked, then struggles to remove it from the door.

"There. Let's get on with it," he grumbles.

The appointment with the lawyer involves the now-familiar routine of standing and waiting in a hallway for hours, but this time, there's only a handful of people in front of us. I'm glad I've brought my note pad along so I can continue recording our experiences in Ukraine, with the hope that one day I can share them with our son, should he show any interest.

Albert spends the day reading his *Cold Mountain* novel, standing directly behind me against the wall. He's silent, so I leave him alone.

Sofia and Iryna have left to attend to other business in town related to Mary and John's adoption file. They promise to return later.

At the end of the day, around 19:00, Yevgeny comes to fetch us. We try to explain to him using hand gestures that we haven't been in to see the lawyer yet, but the driver insists we follow him. Sofia is in the front seat of the car when we climb into the back. She removes her glasses, turns to look at us, and calmly states we'll need to return the following day to see the lawyer.

We camp out again on the second day in the hallway outside the lawyer's office, waiting to receive the one-paragraph statement he's agreed to provide. Sofia and Iryna are inside the anteroom to the lawyer's office, negotiating on our behalf.

I've brought along my three-ring binder to continue reading posts from the Adoption from Ukraine Internet Club. I come across a reference to an article on "Using Respectful Adoption Language" by Patricia Irwin Johnston, the author of several books about infertility and adoption. She notes:

"Though in adoption parent and child are linked by love and law, the fact that they are not connected by blood has often meant that some people are unwilling to acknowledge their relationship as genuine and permanent. Thus they use qualifiers ("This is Bill's adopted son") in situations where they would not dream of doing so in a non-adoptive family ("This is Bill's birth-control-failure son" or "This is Mary's caesarean-section daughter.")

They tend not to assign a full and permanent relationship to persons related through adoption ("Do you have any children of your own?" or "Have you ever met your real mother" or "Are they natural brothers and sisters?") They assume that adoptive relationships are tentative.

The author asserts that adoption is one way to join a family, and an adopted child deserves as much respect in how they are described as any other family member. Irwin Johnson suggests people need to think and speak positively about adoption because it is a responsible and legitimate way to enrich a family.

"Hey, you realize there's no one else here yet waiting to see the lawyer?" Albert interrupts me.

"Uh, yeah, that's great."

I'm thrilled we're first in line, but after several hours of waiting with no one else falling in behind us, it's clear something is wrong.

The time away from our son is trying. Our Ukrainian consultants are soldiering on. I assume they're taking turns buttering up the lawyer's assistant to try and get us in to see him.

Nearing the end of the second day, I'm ready to break down the lawyer's door. He's emerged now and then from his office, greeting us in the hallway with a shrug. Sofia finally extracts the truth from the lawyer's young assistant.

"We will return. Iryna and I must confer with Yevgeny," Sofia explains, raising her hand to wave as the duo leaves to meet our driver.

Within minutes, Sofia, Iryna, and Yevgeny reappear, their faces hopeful.

"To get your document, we must repair the lawyer's computer," Iryna explains. "The man has been trying to fix it on his own, but it is clear now that a technician is required. Yevgeny has a friend who can do the job. Quick, we must hurry. Yevgeny will carry the equipment."

Our driver carries the lawyer's computer to his car. The processor is fixed in a matter of hours, and the lawyer's printer spits out our letter. I feel bad for the lawyer but don't understand why he didn't previously ask for help. Iryna and Sofia refuse our money to pay for the repairs.

"It was nothing, believe me," Iryna says. "Yevgeny's friend is a helpful person."

With the official document from the lawyer in hand, we propose to drive the attorney home as we've kept him late at his office. The man accepts our offer, and we call it a day.

******

The next morning, Albert and I are joking around in the hotel foyer, backpack in hand and impatient to get to the children's home. The stuffed teddy bear's head is poking out the top side of the backpack's pouch. Sofia descends the stairs and enters the lobby.

"Today, is important for you to visit notary public," Sofia reveals. "Is critical step. Iryna will escort you. You can visit your son at Yolochka later in the afternoon. I have commitment with John and Mary. Best of luck to you!"

Dutifully, Albert and I join Iryna in Yevgeny's car, and our group takes off for the centre of the city.

The notary public's office is a one-room portable wooden building perched on concrete blocks in Simferopol's commercial district. The notary is a polished, jovial lady who tells us through Iryna that she enjoys helping people who are adopting children, and that she is the proud mother of a thirteen-year-old daughter. Photos of her daughter posing in assorted ballet costumes are displayed on a shelf behind the woman's desk. The notary's eyes sparkle when she explains her daughter wants to become a teacher.

We are offered tea before getting down to business. Iryna accepts on behalf of the three of us. My husband and I gladly accept the warm cups and settle into comfortable chairs in a corner of the room.

I try to remain upbeat. I sip my tea, and Albert and I patiently wait for the paperwork process to begin. After a few minutes, Iryna asks us to step forward and provide our passports to the notary. The lady takes them, peers at the documents through her navy-rimmed glasses, and nods to verify that my husband and I indeed look like the people in the photos. Iryna then shoos us away and says we will be called upon when needed.

Albert and I slump back down on the chairs. Here we are, once again sitting and waiting while people converse about us in a foreign language. We have to make the best of it, because our Ukrainian consultants are doing whatever they can to move things along for us.

Albert and I talk about how his three daughters back home in Canada are doing, how school might be going, and we flip through our family photo album together. We try to agree on the most romantic date we enjoyed together, what each of us ordered in the restaurant on the night he presented my engagement ring, and recall the first time I met his daughters when we all had dinner together at Red Lobster in downtown Toronto. We try not to let the boredom of waiting get us down.

Iryna swiftly handles the document notarization. Several sheets are officially stamped, each with a thump. The translator then looks back in our direction, stands up, and asks us to step outside. I wonder if she's about to scold us for horsing around too loudly, but Iryna has an important question to ask.

"What is the name for your boy? Please provide it to me. We have ten minutes left before we must leave to submit these papers along with one more to the regional court. Otherwise, we will need to wait a month before we can apply for another court date."

Albert and I look at each other, stunned, and burst out laughing.

"This is not a joke. I will return shortly for the name," Iryna says.

The timing of our translator's request does not go unnoticed. We've been sitting around in hallways for days. Iryna could have told us earlier that we needed to make a definitive decision on our son's name by today. We've been deliberating for months on girls and boys names, but have not yet found common ground. The fact that we're given ten minutes to choose the name our son will carry for the rest of his life is nerve wracking, to say the least.

"We can do this," Albert says, trying to hide the surprised look on his face.

I grab my husband's backpack and retrieve my notes containing my top choices for boys' names. Albert groans, as he knows what's coming.

"Please listen to me," I say. "Don't pre-judge. I love the name 'Georg.' It was Captain von Trapp's first name in my favorite movie, *The Sound of Music*. It connects me to memories of my childhood, and it sounds beautiful. I would also be happy with Helmut, or what about Knut?"

"Are you kidding? Forget the Danish and German names," Albert snorts. "He'll be a laughing stock at school. Pick something less complicated and easy to pronounce. It has to be a name that will resonate in any language, and especially in English or Latvian."

"With a last name like 'Upeslacis,' nothing will be easy to pronounce," I respond.

"Go. Do it. Check the bag. Where is *my* list?" my husband asks.

"I can't keep track of your stuff," I reply. "If you don't have your list handy, that's on you. So, I agree the name should be short and not complicated; one or two syllables would be good. Our last name has four. His first name should be short because it will take our boy forever to learn to write the last name. What about Arnis? That's a nice Latvian name, and it was my uncle's name. He was a kind man. Or, how about Einars?"

"No. They don't suit him. Our boy needs a more solid name, something that conveys his inner strength."

"Well … what about … Erik? That works in any language and it sounds very sturdy. Erik."

"Are you thinking of my nephew, Erik, in Toronto?"

"I wasn't thinking specifically of him, no, but your nephew is smart and he works hard. It's a great name. Easy in any language; our son suits the name perfectly."

"Yeah. Erik. It should be Erik Upeslacis. I like the sound of that," Albert says, clapping his hands together.

"So, for the second and third names? We said we'd go with Jānis, my father's first name, and Viktors, your dad's first name; that way he takes both grandfathers' names."

"Yes. Alright, it's done," Albert concludes. "Let's tell Iryna."

There is a concise but heated discussion with our translator about the second and third names we've chosen for Erik. Iryna reveals that in Ukraine a son takes a component of his father's name, known as a "patronym". She proposes that the second name of our son be officially registered as Albert. We tell Iryna that in Canada this is not common practice, and that it's important for our son to take both grandfathers' names. We express our deep respect for Ukrainian traditions, but remind her we want to honour both of our families through our son's names.

Beads of sweat form on Iryna's forehead. The translator only has a few minutes left to convey our wishes to the notary public. The notary purses her lips while Iryna tranquilly delivers our argument. I raise my hands in a praying motion, smiling at the notary. "Please," I'm conveying to her.

The woman is easygoing and does not seek to rally her position any further. We offer to drive the notary to her late afternoon appointment as we're pressed for time and need to get to the court. She's grateful for the offer of a ride, given that she's sporting four-inch heels. The last sheet of paper is completed, stamped, and notarized and the package is handed to Iryna to submit.

Yevgeny burns rubber as we exit the parking lot. We make it to the courthouse in three minutes flat, as it's literally a block away. Iryna runs in to try and meet the deadline to apply for a preliminary court date with the chief justice of the region of Simferopol. She's back within minutes.

"We met the deadline," Iryna says, collapsing into the front seat of the car. Yevgeny drops the notary public off at a restaurant in town and we depart for the children's home.

My husband and I are only allowed one hour with our son at Yolochka, as we're later than usual to arrive for the scheduled afternoon parental visit. We decide to remain indoors for the visit.

I wonder out loud how Erik will react to seeing us when we haven't been at the home for days.

"Do not worry. Young children have no sense of time," Iryna assures me. "Your boy has no idea how long it's been since you were here."

Yevgeny drops us off at the Yolochka front entrance. Iryna says the driver will back on his own to retrieve us as she will be returning to the hotel to rest before dinner.

The caregivers in Erik's room are unusually cool. None of them hurry to greet us when we arrive at the doorway of the anteroom to S-11, nor does anyone crack a smile.

I suppose they're wondering why we haven't come to spend any time with our son for days. I try to explain to the ladies with hand gestures as to where we've been, but they obviously don't understand. A red-headed caregiver finally goes to fetch Erik from the living space.

She hands Erik to me abruptly, allowing his legs to dangle underneath her hands. I scoop my son up in my arms and kiss him. He glances timidly at me for a moment, and then hugs me tight. Albert kisses Erik's head.

"Erik, it's Papa and Mamma. Let's go for a walk in the building!"

As soon as we step into the hallway, Erik is angling to remove the backpack from my husband's back.

"This is going to be interesting," I say. "Where can we go to sneak some food to our son? This place is crawling with the white-coat ladies."

"We'll find a back stairwell, with no one around. You can feed him and I'll be the lookout."

"Okay. Don't forget to show him the bear."

"The bear can wait."

******

On the drive back to our hotel after feeding and spending time with Erik, Albert asks Yevgeny if he could make a short detour to Simferopol's commercial district so we could send some emails. The chauffeur obliges us.

At the internet cafe, Albert reads and replies to work and family emails. Afterwards, I compose an email asking our relatives to guess our son's first, second and third names. We attach to the email an electronic photo of Erik that Albert got a copy shop to convert into an email-friendly format. The prize for correctly guessing our son's name? One-on-one time with our boy.

With the group guessing contest email sent, we stop at a green grocer to buy provisions for cheese sandwiches, head back to Yevgeny's car, and, back at the Svoboda, retire to our room for the evening.

My husband clicks on the TV. We watch part of a soccer match on BBC, consume the cheese sandwiches, and ready for sleep.

"I love Erik's name," I tell my husband, climbing into bed.

"I'm pretty sure there was a Viking explorer named Erik the Red," Albert responds, yawning. "We've given our son a really great name. You have to be fearless with a sense of adventure if you're going to be an explorer."

"Erik has already proved he's strong and brave," I respond. "To survive and thrive in a children's home, you have to be a fighter with a will to overcome."

With that, my husband is snoring, and I'm not far behind in falling asleep.

The Canadian Doctor

The wait staff of the Svoboda dining room have come to accept that the North Americans in our group are not accustomed to a morning meal of stewed meat, cabbage, or roasted garlic potatoes.

We are now regularly offered bowls of cream of wheat porridge or fried eggs. Sometimes the meal includes a slice of cheese and whole grain bread, too, and that's fine with us, as we keep the bread and cheese for Erik.

When given the opportunity to choose, Albert and I use hand signals to request eggs over easy, or hold up a spoon to order porridge. One breakfast item is oddly denied us: individual containers of fruit yoghurt are set out on some tables in the dining room that we are apparently not permitted to occupy. We never see anyone seated at those tables, but the Svoboda appears ready to receive these mysterious guests, should they ever turn up.

This morning our group is seated together, though everyone is busy with their own morning rituals. John and Mary are making plans to go into the city with their driver, Viktor, in search of clothing and other items for their children. Albert scans a local Russian language newspaper for photos that may provide some glimpse of world events. Sofia is forever talking on her cell phone. Iryna counts out an allotment of vitamins and other pills on the white tablecloth.

I've noted from the first day we met that our translator pays close attention to her health. Rail thin with pale skin and frigid hands, I wonder where Iryna summons the energy to withstand the demands of dealing with functionaries who regularly employ intimidation, stalling, and other tactics.

When pressed for an explanation of her lack of appetite and the daily ingestion of pills, Iryna shrugs it off as an allergy issue that will in time be resolved.

"I will be fine. Thank you; your concern is appreciated but unnecessary."

The translator swallows a handful of pills, and washes them down with tea. I finish my bowl of porridge and see that our group is ready to leave. Iryna removes a small gold case from her purse, applies red lipstick, and puckers up into the tiny mirror on the case.

"See? I look better."

Discussing Iryna's health reminds me of our son's medical assessment, which Dr. Bohdan has undertaken to complete.

"Has the report on Erik's health been sent to the Canadian doctor in Vienna for review?" I ask Iryna.

Sofia has a sixth sense for joining a conversation at the right moment. She closes the lid on her mobile and tells me she's put a call in to Svitlana Korolenko at the Embassy of Canada in Kyiv to make sure Dr. Bohdan's report has been received in Vienna.

"So, they've got it, then?" Albert asks.

"This is what I am hoping," Sofia assures us. "Svitlana not call me back yet. Dr. Bohdan personally sent package by courier last week. It must be in Vienna by now. I will have answer later today. Svitlana is aware of the urgency of this request."

Prior to our trip to Ukraine, our Toronto adoption agent, Laryssa, told my husband and I about a Canadian physician based in Vienna whose job it is to approve medical assessments of prospective adoptive children, including those from Ukraine. Assigned to the Embassy of Canada in Vienna, this individual supervises files pertaining to people wishing to immigrate to Canada from several European countries. The doctor is tasked with approving or denying entry to Canada.

I'm not worried about Canadian medical clearance for our son. Dr. Bohdan has explained that some of the data in Erik's original medical file seems to be in error. He conjectures the material may have been presented in a certain manner so as to ensure a particular level of public funding for the children's home from the government of Ukraine, as support is granted to a facility based on the health status of its residents. Another possible reason is that the original assessment was done in a hurry and the conclusions are simply inaccurate.

I know our son does not suffer from hydrocephalus, the serious condition that is mentioned in his medical file. Hydrocephalus is an abnormal build-up of water on the brain that potentially damages or destroys cell tissue. Dr. Bohdan has assured Albert and I that the diagnosis was in error and would have no bearing on the Canadian review. Children with water on the brain have an enlarged head that is pronounced, and the condition can lead to serious problems in brain function.

Our son's appearance is normal, and he responds to verbal and physical stimuli appropriate to his age and circumstances.

On the drive to the children's home to visit our son, Iryna is scribbling some words on small pieces of paper. One side of each paper has writing in English; the other, in Russian. Each paper corresponds to a location that Yevgeny regularly shepherds us to and from: Yolochka; the Uzbek restaurant; the Svoboda hotel; the open-air market; and the internet cafe in the commercial walking district. This will free up Iryna and Sofia to conduct other business in Simferopol while we go about our own routine.

Albert takes the papers from Iryna and zips them into the pocket of his backpack. We're not the least bit concerned about managing Yevgeny on our own. He knows when we need to be transported to a location, and always arrives on time. At $25 USD per day, our driver is well worth the investment.

It feels great to be back at the children's home for a morning visit, and despite the cold temperature, my husband and I are determined to enjoy an outing with our son in the forest.

At the entrance to the S-11 living room, Erik looks relieved to see us. He drops the pair of shoes he's playing with at the back of the room and runs towards us, arms outstretched.

"Hi sweetie, how's mommy's boy?" I say in Latvian, hugging my son. "Erik, are you ready to go outside? Daddy and I brought you a nice warm snowsuit to wear." My boy holds me tight.

"It's a nice day, let's go and play," Albert says, stroking Erik's head back and forth. "We'll dress now for the outdoors."

I put the yellow snowsuit on our son that we've brought with us from Canada. It's a bit loose, but otherwise fits well.

Albert lifts Erik up on the counter above the cubbyholes, and exchanges our son's ill-fitting shoes for his new boots. Albert ties the laces in double knots, as they are very long.

"Here you go, son," my husband says. "Every time we visit, we'll bring you these boots. And when we leave to go home to Canada, the three of us together, you'll never have to wear ill-fitting shoes or boots again."

Erik takes his time staring down at the boots. He smacks his feet together, looks up at Albert, then at me, and cracks a wide smile. "Meh! Meh!" he says. "Dhizz!" I notice he has a bottom tooth coming in.

The three of us enjoy a magical picnic in the forest despite the increasingly chilly temperature. I'm making good use of my thermal underclothing.

Our son's appetite is voracious, as he finishes all of the provisions we've brought, including and nearly downing, an entire thermos of mint tea, as well.

"Do you think I should give him a granola bar, too?" I ask Albert.

"No. He doesn't have enough teeth to chew it. Those bars are rock hard."

"Okay, but next time we'll need to bring more food. Yevgeny could help us find a place we can buy some meat, fish, or fruit."

After the picnic, we play hide-and-go-seek in the woods. Erik and I find a spot behind a clump of trees where we crouch down while Albert counts to ten out loud and comes to find us. When we're caught, Erik squeals in glee, points at my husband, and says, "Ooorh! Ooorh!"

We repeat the game several times, then chase our son up and down the small hill leading back to the children's home. When it's time to return inside the building, Erik refuses to get in the stroller. He runs away from the buggy as fast as he can, and when Albert catches him to put him back in, Erik becomes agitated.

"Sorry, son. We have to go back but we'll see you again right after lunch." My husband's tone is definitive but kind.

I may have blinders on, but I struggle to see any "red flags" regarding my son's behaviour which could point to future problems we may need to address. It's natural that a boy would want to keep playing with his parents, who are showering him with attention, rather than go back inside to the children's home.

******

Albert and I have some time before the afternoon Yolochka visit to rest at our hotel. While my husband takes a nap, I revisit my adoption information binder once again.

There's a discussion thread about child rearing and how children must be seen as individuals who will have different responses to care and attention they receive. A "one size fits all" approach is wrong. One child may respond to something a certain way and another will react differently. What works for one person may not work for the next.

There is reference made as to how, in developmental psychology, there is always controversy and debate. Without detailed clinical trials it's hard to prove or disprove treatments and methods. Add to that the personal backgrounds and biases of clinicians. So how to know what is best for one specific child?

Anything can happen to a person at any given time that requires a family to rally support. Whether a newly adopted child or an aging parent, having a positive attitude can greatly influence the outcome. Whatever the future holds for our family, I'm certain we'll will work it out together with great love and respect for the individual(s) involved.

The afternoon children's home visit with Erik is indoors, as the temperature has become very cold. Leaving the anteroom to S-11 with our son, my husband and I look for a quiet area where we can read to our boy and show him some children's books we've brought from Canada.

We find a space at the end of a passageway under a staircase where a square rug is positioned on the floor beside a large armchair. We put my husband's backpack, and our coats, on the chair, and the three of us sit down together on the rug. I place a few books on the carpet for our son to enjoy while he eats cookies.

Erik consumes a handful of the sweets. He's fascinated by a tactile book about farm animals. He runs his hand across a lamb's woolly coat, squeezes a duck's beak, and pulls a horse's tail. Albert and I point to the creatures in the book and make noises approximating them.

"The duck says, 'quack, quack'!" Albert says.

"The cow says, 'moo'!" I join in. "The lamb says, "baa'!"

Erik smacks his hands together in glee, and flips the pages of the book back to the beginning so we can reread the book.

Out of nowhere, a pudgy, white-coated caregiver scoops Erik up in her arms and starts yelling at us. She points to the rug, shakes her head and waves her index finger to inform us we're not allowed to let our son sit on the carpet, which is on top of the concrete floor. I arrive at this conclusion once the caregiver lifts the carpet to show us the concrete underneath.

My husband and I both shrug, and the woman becomes even more annoyed. Additional yelling ensues. Whatever the lady is saying, we understand she is insisting we get up off the carpet; no one is apparently allowed to sit on it.

When we stand up, the woman hands Erik back to me.

"*Nyet*," she exclaims. "*Nyet!*"

The caregiver finally realizes we are genuinely perplexed. She grunts loudly, turns on her heels and disappears down the hallway.

"You realize that in the room where Erik lives the children all sit and crawl on cold linoleum flooring, and none of the caregivers ever make them get up," I say to my husband.

"Well, the woman wanted to make us feel bad, for whatever reason."

Despite the odd encounter with the caregiver, my husband and I try to remain upbeat.

As we exit the children's home at the end of the day, Albert says, "Hey, let's drop by the internet cafe to catch up on what's happening at home and also see if any family members have correctly guessed Erik's names."

"Great idea."

"Yevgeny, internet cafe?" my husband asks, climbing in to the car.

"*Da*."

"*Spasibo*." Albert's pronunciation of the word impresses me.

At the internet cafe, while my husband responds to his daughters' messages and work colleagues' email requests, I scan responses to the "guess our son's names" contest.

The family member who is closest to correctly identifying Erik's names is my American cousin who works for the United Nations Development Program in Europe. He correctly estimated that my Dad's name (Jānis) and Albert's father's name (Viktors) would be included among our son's names; but he thought one of them would be the first name. While no one guessed Erik as the first name, my American cousin is crowned the winner.

"Well, two out of three is pretty darn good," my husband admits.

"You bet!" I exclaim. "Not that I'm gloating about the intellectual prowess of my family ..."

Counting Down the Days

Our Ukrainian consultants are making good progress on the adoption procedures with local and regional officials in Simferopol, as my husband and I recently gave our facilitator power of attorney to act on our behalf.

Most mornings after dropping us off at the children's home to visit our son, Sofia and Iryna now head downtown with the chauffeurs, Yevgeny and Viktor. Documents are processed and notarized, and the next round of appointments is booked. I love this approach, as it relieves Albert and I from having to physically wait around in the hallways of Simferopol's municipal and regional offices. Most importantly, we can spend precious time with our son.

Erik is beginning to accept that my husband and I are two people who visit him often and have some connection to him. While in the first days he was fearful and hesitant, over time he has become comfortable with us and enjoys our company. Now when we arrive at his room in Yolochka, he's happy and ready to leave with us and have fun.

Almost by accident, we bonded with our son by offering him food. Erik's priority is getting to the goodies as quickly as possible. He is, after all, malnourished and hungry. My husband and I are making every effort to help him gain weight and become physically and mentally stronger.

We conjecture that before our arrival our son was not allowed to ever play freely outdoors, even though the moderate climate of Simferopol presents good conditions for children to be outside. On our walks around the grounds or in the nearby forest, we don't see any children roaming or running around unless they're with the parents who are in the process of adopting them.

We've observed the white-coat ladies pushing children in double and triple strollers on the grounds. But we've yet to hear the sound of children's laughter, playground banter, the clanging of swings, or creaking of see-saws.

As the days and weeks have passed, Erik has gained weight and become increasingly energetic. He makes all kinds of wonderful sounds, even humming and singing. His voice is sweet and lilting.

Some afternoons when it's too cold or rainy for an outdoor walk, we set up a play zone on one of the area rugs at the back of the second-floor hallway at the children's home. Mary and John join us with their children. All three kids are blossoming, behaving more and more like everyday youngsters, smiling and busying themselves with the books and toys we bring them, including the teddy bear, and Erik is even starting to interact with the other two children.

We've now met several couples adopting children from Yolochka. As the weather has grown colder, some days there are more than twenty couples marching the hallways with their sons and daughters at any one time.

Some people we've encountered from the United States have chosen to adopt children who will need serious medical attention and/or significant psychotherapy over the long term. I wish I could say I'm up to that type of challenge, but I'm relieved to not have to make such a difficult choice.

I am in awe of people who have the desire and means to adopt a gravely ill or disabled child, or one who is suffering from acute psychological trauma. There is a special place in heaven for these people. I salute them.

One couple from Mississippi we've met at the children's home, a nurse and businessman, have their heart set on adopting a three-year-old girl with two broken legs. We learned from the couple that the girl's biological mother was responsible for deliberately breaking the child's legs and burning her body in numerous places with lit cigarettes. Some afternoons we hear the girl's tortured screams in the Yolochka hallway or outside in the nearby forest. It happens when the adoptive mother tries to approach her daughter. The girl will only allow the adoptive father to touch or hold her; she is terrified of women.

We've also met couples from Germany, Spain, and Italy, but the Europeans are more reserved than us, so they don't engage as easily in open conversations as we do.

Nonetheless, I feel a special kinship with all the people adopting children from Yolochka. Apart from devoting as much time as possible to our children, we are all tackling various levels of bureaucracy, trying to fix a court date, working on getting our children's medical clearance, and counting down to the end of the "waiting period," a mandatory time at the conclusion of an international adoption that allows for a biological parent to make a last-ditch effort in claiming their offspring before the child is allowed to leave the country forever. The vast majority of biological parents do not reclaim their child at the last minute, but the possibility remains and is obviously respected.

Albert and I are making the best of the several weeks we are spending in Simferopol together with our son. It allows Erik to get to know us, learn to trust us, and understand that we care about him. It is no small feat for a child who has been denied the affection of parents and family to open their heart and embrace love.

While the physical coldness, darkness and challenging living conditions of Yolochka cause me concern, I believe the institution is something of a miracle. The children's home staff are caring for their country's most vulnerable children in the best way they know how and with the limited resources available to them. They help create families, and this provides children and adoptive parents the immeasurable gift of love and belonging.

Whenever I question the excruciating bleakness of the Yolochka hallways and rooms, Erik instinctively squeezes my hand, reminding me of his generous, loving presence. As winter has come and we are spending more time indoors, Albert and I take turns carrying our son in the hallway while he is teething and fussing from the pain. We sing Latvian folk songs to our boy, and they calm him.

On a sunny morning, the black-and-white Yolochka cats are lazing about on the front steps as my husband and I approach the main door. One hangs her tail over the edge of a step, another lies fully on her side, purring, and the third is curled into a ball.

Albert and I carefully step around the kitties, and I gingerly close the main door behind us so as not to startle them. The elderly administrator nods, expressing her appreciation for my not slamming the door. I note her bright orange cap as she waves us through.

My husband and I head down the hallway, arriving in the anteroom of our son's living quarters to find Erik dressed and ready to go outside. His caregiver seems pleased that our son is keen to be with us and points to the stroller. She disappears back into the children's living space.

Outside, the air is frigid and the ground is dry. We head for the forest; Erik eats along the way. Once out of the stroller, he grabs a handful of dried pine needles, twigs, and leaves, and tosses them up in the air.

"Dhizz!" he giggles.

He throws more clumps of dried ground cover into the air and laughs while dried leaves and decaying bark fall around him. The three of us chase each other in the woods, zig-zagging among the pines, and then we spin around on the spot until we all get dizzy and fall to the ground.

Erik stands up, smiles, and Albert follows him; he chases our boy through the trees. I lay down on the ground, listening to the unadulterated shrieks and laughter of my child echoing in the forest. What a magnificent reverberation.

Albert and I love playing with our son in the forest, and we'll continue to enjoy these special moments together as long as weather permits us to be outdoors. In the woods, Erik comes alive. It's become our sacred place, where no one is watching or telling us what to do.

When it's time to return to the children's residence, Erik allows me to hold his hand and walk with him all the way back while Albert pushes the carriage.

Exploring the woods with our son, feeding him, allowing him to run and jump and hide among nature's glory, is exhilarating. But the more we get to know Erik, the harder it has become to leave him after each visit.

It hurts to know I can't be with my son whenever I want. I need to hold him, wipe his tears, keep him safe from harm, teach him what I know about life, and help him experience joy and love.

I don't know what happens when a child in Erik's room at the children's home becomes upset. Other than crying out in hunger about vastly inadequate meal portions, or screaming from the physical pain of a freezing cold shower, I haven't seen or heard any children expressing their distress.

When and how does a child residing in Yolochka communicate what they need or want, and how does a caregiver respond? I may never know the answer to these questions. Even if I did, what would it change?

As Yevgeny pulls his sedan away from the children's residence, Albert and I are quiet in the back seat. The chauffeur glances at me through the rear-view mirror. Looking back at him, I wonder what he reads in my face: the warm afterglow of a visit with Erik, or the sorrowful truth of being forcibly separated from my son?

With two more weeks of adoption paperwork and approvals to complete, I choose to remain hopeful and upbeat. It's the only way I can see it through.

December 2000
Week Four

Surprises, Good and Bad

Traffic is stalled on the way back to the Svoboda hotel from an afternoon visit at the children's home. Simferopol is raining cats and dogs. Rush hour has begun in earnest; bus stops are crammed to overflowing.

Sofia, in the front seat beside Yevgeny, is busy writing in her notebook.

"Uh, Sofia, I just remembered," I pipe up. "Did you hear back from Svitlana Korolenko in Kyiv about Dr. Bohdan's medical report on Erik? Did the Canadian doctor in Vienna receive it?"

Sofia stops writing, and turns to look back at us, brushing her blonde bangs away from her eyes. "No, I have not heard

187

back," she replies. "You are correct in pointing this out. I will call Svitlana now, to see if she has an answer."

We soon learn that Svitlana has heard from Vienna. The doctor received the report, but is asking that more tests be done before he can make a final decision on approving Erik's entry to Canada. Svitlana reads the list of analyses requested; Sofia writes them down and reads them back to Svitlana on the phone to confirm the information has been correctly understood.

"There are three tests requiring small blood samples from Erik that the Vienna doctor is asking for," Sofia explains. "Laboratory in Simferopol is equipped to expedite this matter. We will go to Yolochka tomorrow and arrange for tests to be done. Do not worry; this is routine."

Albert asks, "Can we accompany our son to the lab?"

"No, I am sorry," Sofia says. "This is not allowed."

Back at the Svoboda before dinner, there's a large contingent of police cars in the hotel parking lot. My husband and I enter the lobby together with Sofia and inquire at the front desk as to what's going on.

One of the clerks mentions something about Leonid Kuchma, the President of Ukraine. The hotel management has been informed he will be visiting Crimea shortly, hence the police presence.

Albert plops our room key down on the reception desk. He asks Sofia to explain to the front desk clerks that we have difficulty using the key as it frequently gets stuck in our guest room door. We'd like to get a new key, if they have one, or, if not, possibly change rooms.

Sofia conveys the request in a syrupy, fawning tone to the younger clerk, so as not to annoy the lady. The stocky older clerk, hearing the conversation, steps forward. She pushes her chest out as she inches closer to Sofia. Pointing to the cubbyholes behind her housing room keys, the clerk tersely states there are no other available rooms or keys, and suggests we make do. She motions for us to step away from the desk and gives Albert a dirty look.

Before Sofia has translated the conversation, my husband and I already know the outcome; we back down. I understand accommodations in Ukraine may not approximate the modern conveniences of some Canadian hotels. And while my husband is irked about not being able to change rooms, he calms down when I remind him of the charming nature of the hotel and its relative safety and security.

The heating system now kicks in on the coldest nights, so we don't completely freeze in our hotel room, and we have little to complain about, given that the children's home is never heated. While there is a form of toilet paper in our Svoboda bathroom, the Yolochka water closet, located on the second floor of the home, never has any toilet paper, nor is there a sink to wash up in.

Our hotel guest room has a refrigerator in which we can store the food provisions we've purchased to bring to our son, which is convenient. There's a kettle to boil water for the steaming thermos of peppermint tea we carry each day in our backpack. The thermos has come in handy during long stints in hallways or for picnics outside in the forest with Erik. The television in our guest room is reliable and shows daily broadcasts of *Die Welt* from Germany and *BBC World*, both transmitted in English.

Laundry service is practically free. During our time in Simferopol, the young hotel staff who perform this function have been doing an excellent job of washing and pressing our clothes at very reasonable rates. Having John and Mary next door is also a plus as it gives us a sense of not being alone in a foreign country.

Still, it's difficult to accept why Sofia and Iryna have inferior accommodations compared to ours. Their rooms are small. There is no television set in the guest rooms and no refrigerator. We already upgraded the consultants to these rooms from the initial substandard guest rooms they were given for the first days of our stay. It took a week of John prodding the two hotel clerks in his respectable Russian to get them to admit there was no running water whatsoever in the ladies' lodgings. Now at least our Ukrainian consultants can enjoy the same cold or hot showers that we do.

With the day's business concluded, Sofia invites us to dine with her in the tiny cafe a few steps up and to the left off the lobby of our hotel, which she explains is a quick and convenient alternative to the formal Palace hotel dining experience.

We enter the cafe, which is about three square meters in size. It's cozy and warm, with bright red tablecloths on two small tables. Russian cinema posters decorate the walls.

"*Dobryy vecher*"—good evening—the chef says, acknowledging Sofia.

"*Dobryy vecher,*" Sofia retorts, nodding.

As we step up to the counter to order, Sofia explains that two women take turns running the kitchen, seven days a week. It's open for lunch and dinner, and the food is excellent.

I scan the day's dinner offering, which is scrawled in Cyrillic on the blackboard behind the chef. Sofia translates that tonight the lady is serving pan-fried pork with cabbage and carrot salad and pan-fried potatoes.

We watch the chef skillfully prepare the dishes on a small hot plate and cutting board behind the service counter. Freshly grated carrots and shredded cabbage are tossed with chopped garlic, oil, lemon juice and salt. Potatoes are peeled, cut, and fried in a cast iron pan. Substantial pork chops are beaten with a heavy metal cleaver, seasoned, dipped in an egg mixture, breaded,and fried.

Sofia shows us to the corner table, where we sit waiting for the meal that smells delicious. Three platters arrive in short order, and the smiling chef says "*Bon appétit!*" in her best French.

Slicing into her pork chop, Sofia confirms to us the Ukrainian president is due to arrive the following day in Crimea for meetings with regional officials. A massive sweep of Simferopol hotels and other facilities is being undertaken, for security reasons.

"However, this does not concern us," Sofia assuredly states, raising her fork. "Is good to have police in parking lot. They are there for protection."

Our bellies full, our party heads upstairs for the night. Albert and I are exhausted. We turn in before long and barely say goodnight to one another.

Early the next morning, I test the shower nozzle and am pleasantly surprised to feel hot water rushing out. I hop in, quickly use the soap and shampoo, then turn it off. My husband is sound asleep and there's no need to wake him yet.

After showering, I tiptoe into the bedroom with my towel on, combing out my hair. There's a loud knock on the door.

"*Politsiya!*" a man yells. He says some other words, too. "*Politsiya!*" He repeats the other words and bangs on the door again.

I feel my heart skip a beat. My hands tremble. I throw on my dressing gown, grab the guest room key and walk to the door. Carefully turning the key, I rattle and fiddle with it until I can finally free the lock and open the door.

Two machine gun barrels point directly at me; behind them are two uniformed military men. A black-haired woman in a trench coat stands beside the men. Her arm stretches out towards me, palm facing upward.

The woman is yelling at me; something about passports.

"Pardon me?"

"*Pasport!*"

I walk to the bed, rouse Albert and tell him there are men with machine guns and a lady standing at the door apparently demanding our passports.

"Give them to her," he says, his voice gravelly.

I go to the chair by the bed, retrieve our passports from the backpack, walk to the door, and hand them to the lady. She grabs the documents and slams the door shut.

"Oh shit," I say. "What did I just do?"

"You had no choice."

Within seconds, I pick up the phone to dial Sofia's room. The line is dead.

"Perfect," I declare. "We're in Ukraine, a foreign country. I just gave our passports to an angry lady standing beside two guys pointing guns at me, and we have no way of reaching the outside world."

I comb out my hair, blow dry, climb back into bed and crawl in tight against my husband's back.

Less than an hour later, the phone rings. It's Iryna, explaining the military police are conducting a check of guests in our hotel as part of a security sweep in advance of President Kuchma's visit to the region. We are to remain composed. She's hopeful our passports will be returned within a few hours.

Albert and I get dressed, tidy our guest room, and wait.

"Have you read anything about Leonid Kuchma?," I ask my husband as I tie the velvet belt on my sweater into a bow. "Is he possibly a decent guy?"

"Kuchma is completely deferential to Russia. He ran on a promise to *improve* relations with Russia. His support is in the east, which is where we are now, and as you now know, this is where many Russian speakers live. Questions were raised about the media coverage of the most recent election, which seemed weighted to favour Kuchma. What was *that* all about? The current Ukrainian president evidently has no desire to tear Ukraine away from Russia's influence. That's what I think."

"Hmmm. So maybe not the best person to leapfrog Ukraine into a prosperous future?"

"I hope we're both wrong."

After a while, Albert and I tire of waiting and head down to the hotel lobby. Nothing alarming seems to be going on. We exit the Svoboda front door. There are no police cars anywhere. We go to the dining hall and find the rest of our group eating breakfast. No one's feathers appear to be ruffled.

By the time we are clambering into the back of Yevgeny's vehicle and headed for the children's home, a reception desk clerk runs out, handing the driver our passports. I breathe a sigh of relief.

******

It's Saturday night in Simferopol. A man at the Palace hotel restaurant entrance offers to check our coats. He lets us know there's a cover charge this evening due to a special performance. Albert and John look a bit surprised, then split the fee for our party of six and take our coat check tickets.

As we are seated in our usual comfy booth, Anatoly, the server, eagerly describes to our group the "sexy cabaret show" about to unfold.

"I don't think you will see anything like this in Canada," he gushes.

Mary and I look at each other, shaking our heads and shrugging, wondering what kind of spectacle we're about to see. Sofia and Iryna could care less about the show and instead review the menu. Albert and John look happy.

I note to myself the unusually numerous groups of patrons seated throughout the room. Bouquets of fresh flowers wrapped in cellophane have been placed on some of the tables in celebration of specific individuals. Birthdays or anniversaries are likely being marked.

Viktor is anxious to get our dinner choices out of the way before the performers begin the show. Each of us decides to try something new. Viktor writes down the order: Spiced beef. Mushroom dumplings. Marinated chicken. Charred fish. Grilled pork. Yoghurt and tea for Iryna. The server nods approvingly.

Beer for the men in our group arrives quickly. Albert is in heaven, as he's come to appreciate the qualities of the organic Ukrainian brew, free of additives or chemicals. Canadian beer often gives him a headache. Mary, Sofia, and I enjoy juice cocktails.

A toast is made to the women of Ukraine; Sofia and Iryna nod appreciatively. Sofia puts her hands to her heart and expresses thanks for our generosity and the pleasant company she's enjoying during our journey together. Iryna looks a bit fatigued; the bags around her eyes are puffy, but she musters up her usual sparkly smile and the pleasant demeanor which brightens everyone's day.

Anatoly appears at our table, gently informing us there's a slight problem in the kitchen and that once again our dinner orders will be delayed. John acknowledges the comment with a slight grunt; there's no need to elaborate the point.

We're still waiting for dinner to arrive when the room suddenly goes dark. There's a loud drumroll, and, after a few seconds, theatrical lights beam down onto the centre of the room.

Seven young women strut around the dance floor in unitards and colourful skirts. Each sports large feather headgear and a sheer scarf tied at the waist. The stage lights change colour according to the musical beat. The nubile dancers kick their legs ever higher. All seven drop dramatically to the floor in unison, doing perfect splits, arms reaching high.

They get up, twirl around, move their torsos seductively to the music, and run their hands up and down their own bodies, inviting patrons in the room to take notice.

Albert and John crank their necks to watch the girls prance around the room as they slowly remove the scarves from their waists and graze them along the necks, heads, and chests of male patrons in the audience.

As our table is far from the stage area, it takes a while for the performers to reach us. By then, our guys have each snapped numerous photos of the nimble dancers. Two of the ladies glide over to our table. The smallest one, a brown-haired beauty with deep-set green eyes, drags a sheer orange scarf across my husband's face. She pulls it along the top of his head, down around his shoulders, across his chest, and then back over her own body, gyrating seductively in front of him, inviting further exploration. My husband is speechless.

John's performer is a tall blonde with bony shoulders but sizeable breasts. The woman shakes her bosom in front of John's face. She leans in as if to kiss the burly Canuck, but John knows better and moves his head back away from her to avoid contact. The dancer takes John's face in her hands, and shakes her hips forcefully.

The climax of the show is performed in the centre of the dining hall. The girls move closer together and begin dancing wildly in a circle, jerking their wrists up and down and pulsing their hips to a Persian beat. Their heads snap from side to side. As they move, the circle becomes smaller and smaller.

Finally, one dancer is hoisted up to stand on the shoulders of two others. Her legs remain still, but her upper body and arms create a wave effect. The group moves frenetically as the music plays faster and louder, but, in the end, only a drum beat remains. Finally, the girl on the shoulders of the others jumps up, soars past her troupe, and lands straight with her feet on the floor, arms thrust high in the air, and head back. The drumming stops. The dancers form a chorus line, holding hands, and bow low to the audience. The clapping is vigorous.

Shortly thereafter, Anatoly appears with his large platter to present our dinner orders.

"I trust you enjoyed the performance?" The server is grinning.

"Most definitely! Champagne for the table!" Albert spontaneously announces.

"*Bien sûr*. Of course!" John concurs.

Sofia lifts her head to look at John, and smiles.

Court of Simferopol

The Regional Court of Crimea is located at a busy Simferopol street corner. It's a four-storey architectural and historical marvel with elaborately decorated stone moldings. Inside, uniformed police officers, wrought iron prisoners' gates, and humourless justice officials create a stifling and fearful atmosphere.

Albert and I are in the unusual circumstance of going to court because we've requested it. The outcome we anticipate will give us the right to bring our son home to Canada as his legal guardians forever. There is no question; we will be Erik's parents in every sense of the word. So, there's no potential downside to our visit with the judge.

I take my time getting ready for court. I washed my hair the previous evening and set it in rollers, aware that the following day there may be no warm water to wash up in.

Albert has polished my high-heeled boots and his own formal black leather shoes for the occasion. My tartan navy and green wool skirt has been hanging on the bathroom door to loosen any wrinkles, along with my green sweater, allowing the shower steam to flatten any creases. I quickly dress.

Albert inspects his suit in the bathroom mirror, and verifies that our backpack contains our passports, family photo album, and his still camera. Sofia has been preparing the necessary documents on our end and will bring them to the appointment with the judge. As we step into Yevgeny's vehicle, I'm optimistic the day will go well.

"Good morning," Sofia and Iryna say in unison.

"Morning, ladies," Albert cheerily replies.

Yevgeny seems in a hurry as he fights morning traffic. He hits the brakes abruptly at a traffic stop. Sofia speaks to Yevgeny in a hushed tone. We soon arrive at the court building. The Ukrainian consultants scurry out of the car, running across the street toward the courthouse entrance. Albert and I have no idea out what the fuss is about; we're more than an hour early for the appointment.

Yevgeny motions for us to remain in his vehicle.

I put my head back against the car seat. I hate sitting in Yevgeny's car when it's not in motion. The smell of cigarettes and chemical air freshener make me nauseous.

I open the car door and gesture to Albert that I need some air. He follows me outside. We stand beside the vehicle, staring at the court building across the street, and decide to take a short walk. There's a resto-bar nearby. We go in. I'm craving a coffee, but the barman doesn't appear to understand what I want. I point to the small espresso cups and espresso machine behind the bar. The server shakes his finger at me.

We finally settle on bottled water, as the only other option of beverage available in the establishment appears to be alcohol.

"*Voda*," I tell the server. He knows what I mean.

We take a seat in the bar by the window where we can see Yevgeny's car, and watch people go by. Young women push baby carriages, elderly men and women walk arm in arm. Everyone looks content. The biting cold is tempered by a bright morning sun.

Albert and I eventually saunter back to the car. We inquire with Yevgeny using hand signals if Sofia or Iryna have called him on their cell phone.

"*Nyet,*" he responds.

Despite the bitter chill, I'm not ready to sit in the stinky vehicle. We hover near the car outside, hopping occasionally on one foot to try and stay warm, but a fierce breeze starts blowing that becomes increasingly uncomfortable.

Albert checks his watch. Our meeting is half an hour behind schedule. Did we really think it would start on time? We step back into the sedan to warm up. I soon see Iryna sprinting across the street towards us. She leaps into the car.

"There is a slight complication with the schedule, but we will have our meeting with the judge today." With that, she exits the vehicle again and is gone.

A few hours later, our patience running thin, my husband and I are allowed to enter the court building. Iryna leads the way as we hike up the stairs to the fourth-floor judge's chambers. Sofia meets us in the hallway by his office, and we all go in together.

Judge T.F. Yurkovich of the Central District Court of Simferopol has a stern manner but an honest face. The balding Ukrainian explains (through Iryna's translation) the purpose of our meeting is to set a date for the actual court hearing.

Judge Yurkovich queries if we understand the gravity of what we are undertaking. I nearly burst out laughing from nervous energy, but Albert grabs my arm, indicating for me to stay quiet.

"Yes," my husband confidently asserts.

Judge Yurkovich continues, asking if we are ready to take the formal step of becoming Erik's parents. My husband and I look at each other and blurt out "*Tak*! Yes!" simultaneously. The judge cracks a smile. He wants to know if Canada has approved our son for adoption.

Albert and I trade nervous glances. Iryna clears her throat, and translates to the judge that we have every reason to believe Erik will soon be approved by the Canadian government; we are simply waiting on the formality of medical clearance papers to arrive.

Judge Yurkovich sets an expeditious date for the hearing. Sofia looks as though she's about to speak, but relents and remains quiet.

On the drive from the courthouse to the children's home, we discuss the need to accelerate the approval for Erik's medical papers. Sofia says that everything can be worked out, but something doesn't sit right with me.

Inside the main door of the children's home, the front desk clerk lets Iryna know my husband and I will only have an hour's visitation time with our son, given that the dinner hour is fast approaching.

Sofia and Iryna confirm they will meet us back at the front lobby in an hour. In the meantime, they will confer with a Yolochka physician about the results of Erik's blood tests.

Erik looks happy to see us. It's been frustrating to be away from him for most of the day. He skips toward us, arms outstretched and chirping away in his unintelligible language.

I pick up my son and kiss him. I feel him hugging me tight and I savour the moment.

It's dark outside, so my husband and I opt to remain indoors. We put our coats down on a couch at the end of a hall and do the walking tour of the home's main floor with our son. Erik seems agitated that Albert won't remove his backpack and open it, as per the usual routine. My husband and I want to wait until there's a quiet moment where no Yolochka staff are nearby before we give our son any food.

"Can we really get this past the white-coat ladies?" my husband wonders aloud.

We've purchased some type of meat pastry from a cafe for the visit, as we'd like to give Erik healthy food with protein, as opposed to just cookies. When the hallway seems to be free of the staffers, Albert lifts the meat pastry out from his backpack. I put it close to Erik's mouth. He takes a hefty bite just as a Yolochka physician is sauntering by.

The woman grabs the pastry out of my hand and starts speaking rapid-fire at me. She forcefully takes my arm and ushers me down the hall, into S-11. Erik's caregivers are shown what I've done. A heated discussion ensues between the caregivers and the lady who manhandled me. Eventually, the woman allows me to return to the hallway. My son is crying and Albert is holding and rocking him when I get back to them.

By the time we return our son to his room after the visit, one of the head physicians, who speaks a bit of English, is waiting for us. She explains that one of Erik's caregivers will be held to account and will need to write a confessional letter outlining her egregious error in allowing us to provide unauthorized food to our son. This will be a permanent black mark in the woman's employment file. I feel terrible for the trouble we've caused the caregiver, and outraged that the old Soviet system of forcing people to confess to things they didn't do apparently remains in place in Ukraine.

Sofia and Iryna are in no better mood when we meet them in the reception area to return to our hotel. They give us a stern warning not to give Erik anything to eat other than dry cookies.

Albert sighs deeply. He tells me with his eyes that he doesn't care what anybody says, we'll do whatever we think is best to help our son grow stronger and flourish. We can't help it; we grew up in a country where individual freedom and democracy reign supreme. We are free-thinking people who will do what we deem to be in the best interest of our son, within the limits of the law.

On the drive back to the Svoboda hotel, Sofia shares good news. Erik's medical tests reaffirm his good health; she sees no reason for the Vienna physician to stall any further on our son's medical clearance. She's already faxed the test results to Vienna and is hopeful the document will put an end to any doubt about Erik's medical status.

Albert is joyful, his face beaming. "What excellent news, Sofia! Thank you for that."

The next morning at Yolochka, when we're about to take Erik outside, one of his caregivers approaches my husband and I with a document in her hand. The woman's face is flushed;

she looks embarrassed and angry. She shows us the document. I try to explain that I can't read Russian. She pushes it toward me. I feel awful. I take the paper and pretend to read it. What can I say? I know it's not her fault we've been feeding our son what we believe is best because we don't want him to be malnourished anymore.

"I'm sorry," I tell the lady. "I know you had nothing to do with this. We know you're doing your best to take care of Erik, and now there's a blemish in your file. Please, accept my apology."

I sheepishly hand the paper back to the lady.

The woman gives me a disgusted look, and turns away.

Despite the weather turning noticeably harsher, Albert and I are ready to head outdoors. Erik is well bundled up in his snowsuit with a woolen shawl on his lap in the stroller to protect him from the elements.

We head outside. It's so cold, we hurry with the carriage to the forest, give Erik his cheese, juice, and yoghurt, and start a running game to keep warm. I hide with Erik behind a tree. Albert finds us and chases us. We jump up and down, arms in the air, and do jumping jacks.

"Come on, son, try to jump like we are. It's fun!" Albert's voice is booming.

Our son watches the jumping jacks, tries to imitate us, and screams excitedly. We run from tree to tree and laugh.

The temperature is dropping quickly due to a fierce wind; we realize we had better get our child back inside.

At the side entrance leading to the anteroom of S-11, one of Erik's caregivers meets us at the door, takes the stroller from

Albert's arms with Erik inside it, pulls the carriage up into the room, and slams the door in our faces.

We're a good hour from the end of our visitation time. We march to the front of the building and attempt to enter through the reception area. The old woman refuses us entry, her eyes cast downward.

Where are all the other parents with their children? Have they remained inside because of the weather?

We stand outside at the front of the building, hoping Yevgeny might magically appear with his warm car, or Viktor, perhaps, who may be coming to fetch John and Mary early for some reason. The driveway is empty. Snow is beginning to fall in large clumps, and wind is unremittingly blowing white, wet chunks into our faces.

My husband and I walk back around to the rear of the children's home, looking for a possible entry point and try to see if Mary or John might be in any of the rooms. They're not. All of the doors are locked. As we make our way back toward the front of the building, we see a motorcade of black luxury sedans turn into the driveway. Several men get out, one in a police uniform.

Albert and I decide to retreat into the forest, where the tree canopy could possibly provide some protection from the wind. Luckily, we've got our warm thermos of tea, which is nearly full. We share the hot drink in a dense area of the forest and try to keep each other amused.

As time ticks on, I worry about what is really happening at Yolochka. "Do you think it has anything to do with the black-market stuff Laryssa told us about? Did the police possibly catch someone trying to sell or buy a child?"

"Who knows? We need to stay out of it," Albert says, shivering. "We don't know anything, and it's obvious, the children's home staff don't want us anywhere near the building right now."

At 11:30 sharp, when the morning visit time ends, we rush to the Yolochka main entrance. Within a few moments, Yevgeny's car rolls into the driveway.

The chauffeur drops us at the usual Uzbek restaurant for lunch. Sofia, Iryna, John, and Mary are already inside sipping hot soup.

"Ah. Here you are," Sofia chuckles, offering us the two empty seats beside her.

My husband is not happy. He asks why we were forced out from the children's home into the freezing cold.

"Oh, I must apologize," Sofia calmly states, her voice wavering slightly. "There is a visitation by prosecutor's office from Kyiv. It is best not to be seen in these moments."

What I really want to say to Sofia, but don't, is that maybe my husband and I were made to remain outside in the cold as payback for not following the rules, for ignoring the caregivers' instructions about what type of food we're allowed to give our son. I may not speak Russian, but I know there are many ways to get a point across.

The lunch conversation is sparse. My husband and I both order chicken soup with dill and dark rye bread and Nescafe with milk. I cradle the steaming soup bowl with my frigid hands to warm up. I swallow a big spoonful; it warms me instantly.

Across from us, John and Mary are discussing the medical clearance for their children.

"Sorry to jump in on your conversation," Albert speaks up, "but if I hear correctly, what you're talking about is not far off from our own situation. We're coming down to the wire to get Erik's medical documents done before the final court date. Sofia, can you enlighten us?"

The consultant raises her hands, gesturing for everyone to calm down.

"Please, everything is being addressed. The medical clearance documents are being processed. I would like to propose that the four of you visit the commercial centre in Simferopol this afternoon. With the prosecutor's visit to Yolochka, all family visits are cancelled for the rest of today. Iryna and I will attend to the paperwork and continue to move things forward on your adoption files."

Together with John and Mary, Albert and I squeeze into Yevgeny's vehicle.

The driver stops his vehicle near the commercial pedestrian district and shows on his watch that he'll return to the same location in three hours' time. We nod our agreement.

John and Mary take off on their own looking for a German electronics store. My husband and I head to the internet cafe.

After addressing some emails, we take our time exploring the entire shopping district, which encompasses several city blocks, walking briskly to try and stay warm.

We stop in front of a store where a couple of street musicians are playing American jazz music. Albert drops a pile of hryvnias into the nearby open trombone case. The older man of the duo nods his thanks.

Further down the block, there's a historic church, where a couple has just gotten married. The young bride poses amiably for photos in a weightless tulle gown on the steps of the church, despite the brutally cold outdoor temperature. The groom gazes dreamily at his bride in his dark wool wedding jacket adorned with shiny silver buttons.

A few streets over, we come upon a wide square with a larger-than-life bronze statue of Vladimir Lenin, the brutal Russian leader who founded the Soviet empire.

In 1917 Lenin said, "The state is an institution built up for the sake of exercising violence."

I'm trying to imagine why an independent Ukraine has not yet toppled the Lenin statue and replaced it with a true Ukrainian hero. Albert notes that this is an example of Russia maintaining influence over a recently independent people who should be allowed to freely forge their own future, rather than continue to bow and scrape to those who enslaved them.

"If you'll remember, just last year when we were in Latvia, we saw Soviet monuments that remained in place," my husband recounts. "Living beside Russia is a daunting reality, even when the army has left and gone home. And besides, there are probably still hundreds, or even thousands, of Soviet leaders' monuments dotted throughout Ukraine."

"How ridiculous," I say.

"Well, it's probably a deliberate political decision Ukraine has made to stay on good terms with its former occupier. Plus, with all the Russian speakers who remain in this country, you can't suddenly bulldoze all the remnants of the past regime. Ukraine will evolve as a free country over time."

Further on our walk, at the corner of a major intersection, is a historic building housing a department store. We enter the building through an enormous, etched glass-and-wood door. Inside, at the top of a wide, winding staircase, is a children's section.

Colourful, fleece-lined mitten-and-hat collections are displayed. We choose one set for each child residing in Erik's room, hoping they'll help the kids stay warm through the winter. We also buy an assortment of soft corduroy pants, sweat pants, and cozy sweaters in Erik's size.

Shelves with developmental toys offer whimsical picture blocks and oversize numbers, soft floor mats with animal drawings, and extra-large fantasy figure puzzles children could have fun with. We purchase a variety of toys for the S-11 children's room, in the hope that the caregivers will let the children play with them.

Prosecutor's Visit

Yaroslav Kyrylo Mazur, the perfumed children's home director, is standing in the Yolochka front lobby as we cross the threshold into the children's home for our morning visit. He smiles uneasily and bows his head, briefly acknowledging us.

The elderly reception area gatekeeper looks surprisingly stylish in an up-to-the-minute navy sweater with a silver layered necklace and freshly coiffed hair. Her peach lipstick and blush round out her professional appearance. What the heck is going on?

The old lady hastily signals us through, refraining from showing any hint of familiarity or amity. On the way to Erik's living space, I note the hallway has a fresh, pleasing smell, like gently scented pine cleaner. Every light socket has been fitted with a working lightbulb with the effect of vibrantly illuminating the usually dim passages. The floor is so clean it shines. I feel a warmth that's previously eluded me in the children's home. Soon, I realize there is heat is coming from the radiators along the wall, which were previously not turned on.

When we get to the anteroom of S-11, I can see that the floor has a fresh carpeted runner. A new painting of a dog and cat is displayed on the wall.

Inside the children's living area, my jaw drops. A sizeable Persian rug has been laid out on the floor. Toys are scattered all over the carpet. The children are gathered on the rug, mesmerized by the playthings. Erik proudly holds up a bright green truck, showing us what he's got, and spins one of the wheels with his fingers.

"Ooorh!"

Even the hobbyhorse boy and headbanger sit attentively on the carpet, participating in the movable feast of trucks, cars, dolls, and stacking blocks. A caregiver is down on her knees, interacting with her charges and showing them how to assemble the blocks.

What exactly transpired during the prosecutor's visit? My husband and I conjecture he's still in town, as Mazur is obviously expecting someone, the building is spotless, spaces are warm and newly redecorated, and workers are on their best behaviour.

Erik hums to himself in the carriage as we head outside for the morning outing. Turning a corner of the Yolochka building, we nearly collide with the children's home director and a young man in a long formal coat walking the grounds. Is this the Kyiv prosecutor? Mazur acknowledges us with a brief "*Hallo*," his attempt to speak English, while the gentleman alongside him barely tips his hat in our direction.

Albert pushes the stroller up and down the small hill towards the forest. Erik screeches merrily as my husband pretends to almost tip the buggy over several times. We meet a couple in the forest taking turns carrying a little girl on their arms—the Spaniards. As we don't know much Spanish beyond, "*Hola*," I say hello and wave as we pass them.

Albert steers around the woods, looking for a good place to picnic. When the wheels of the stroller stop turning, Erik reaches his arms up to be lifted out. I pick him up and place him down on the ground. He immediately rushes to the backpack, trying to pull it off Albert's back.

Each visit, we seek to bring more provisions, depending on what we can access—cheese, yoghurt, bread, and juice, along with the dry cookies preferred by the orphanage staff. Whatever is in the backpack, our son consumes as though he hasn't had a meal in weeks.

After playing in the woods, I help Erik back in the stroller, and we slowly make our way to the side entrance of the children's home. My son holds my hand while my husband pushes the carriage. The pattern is now well established, and we repeat it nearly every day, weather permitting.

Erik is becoming more and more attached to us. I feel a huge sense of relief, as some of the literature given to us by Laryssa, our Toronto adoption agent, suggests that certain children from an institutional setting initially prefer one parent over the other. Albert and I have consciously tried and continue to do everything equally with Erik. We spend as much time as is allowed together for the three of us, hoping this may negate any preference our son may feel towards one of us.

As we depart Yolochka, Yevgeny waves to us from his car in the driveway to hurry up and get in. Sofia is on her cell phone in the front seat beside him. As we wiggle into the back seat, Sofia ends her call. Yevgeny steers through the gate of the children's home and we head towards the centre of town.

"Today we will all go to Tatar restaurant for lunch," Sofia explains. "The three of us, plus Mary and John, Iryna, and drivers come too. This is unique cultural experience. But first I must inform you of some news." Sofia removes her reading glasses and returns them to their case. She snaps the case shut.

"The test results for Erik we faxed from Simferopol to Vienna six days ago were not received by doctor in Vienna."

"Pardon me?" my husband exclaims, looking somewhat exasperated.

"Fax was not successful. Canadian machine was turned off. We did send again today."

"Thank you," Albert states in monotone.

The deadline for our court date is fast approaching. I have a sick feeling in my stomach that we may run out of time waiting for Canada to approve Erik's health assessment before our hearing date with the Ukrainian judge.

I ask Sofia if she could connect with Svitlana in Kyiv to try and move things along with the Vienna doctor and let her know we urgently need Erik's medical clearance. The facilitator punches in the number on her phone and calls Svitlana. I try to decipher what's being said. Whatever it is, Sofia does not look happy. I hear her say, "*Ni*" a few times, meaning something is not happening.

"We have problem. Vienna doctor go on vacation. Not back for ten days."

Our two chauffeurs have parked their cars side-by-side in front of a vast red tent in a quiet area of Simferopol.

"We are here. Tatar restaurant."

Sofia is first out of the car and opens the back door for me. Albert exits from the other side.

The eating establishment is fully outdoors, under the tent. There's no floor, just dirt, stones and mud beneath our feet.

An immense wood stove is burning in the heart of the windswept eatery, strategically placed so that smoke can rise up and out the huge air hole at the apex.

We are led to a picnic bench in the middle of the establishment, surrounded by noisy locals. Yevgeny and Viktor have accepted Sofia's invitation to join us. As we sit, I notice for the first time how broad-shouldered the two men are. Seated across from me, they reveal their sculpted, muscular arms when they remove their leather jackets.

Moustached male servers in traditional baggy Tatar pants and cloaks with black *kalpak* lambskin headgear balance silver trays with samovars and small teacups as they move gracefully from table to table. The aroma of succulent grilled lamb, onions and garlic rouses my taste buds.

I conclude that this unique culinary excursion must be a diversionary tactic by Sofia to minimize the distress my husband and I may be feeling about the medical clearance quagmire. If that's the case, it's working.

Our drivers are ethnic Crimean Tatars who are intimately familiar with the menu, as well as being friends of the establishment's owner. Yevgeny excitedly orders for us all.

Piping hot tea arrives momentarily and is poured by a waiter from a great height into small cups with precision.

Yevgeny commands an appetizer consisting of rolled meat in vinegar with pickled onions. Fish soup with lemon and greens arrive next, followed by vegetable patties stuffed with pumpkin, carrot, and cabbage, meat turnovers with spicy filling, and lamb shish kebab. It's far too much food for a midday meal, but we somehow manage not to leave a crumb.

Save for our table, all of the restaurant patrons are smoking while dining. Yevgeny and Viktor savour their after-lunch cigarettes and order several more rounds of tea.

I'm lethargic after the meal, but at the same time, determined to resolve Erik's file with the Canadian government. I ask Yevgeny to make a stop at our hotel before returning to Yolochka for the afternoon visit.

From our hotel guest room, Albert and I telephone Laryssa in Canada. I ask if she might be able to reach any of her federal government contacts in Ottawa who engage with international adoption cases to see if there's any way to expedite our case. We also ask if she could inquire with Svitlana Korolenko of the Embassy of Canada in Kyiv, to determine what action she might recommend. Laryssa agrees to do what she can, and promises to email a reply.

Back at Yolochka for the afternoon visit, the children's home has reverted to its previous disheartening state.

The heat is turned off. Hallways are dim and silent. Rugs, wall hangings and toys have all been removed from room S-11, and locked in whatever vault they came from. The hobbyhorse rider is back in his saddle, and the headbanger, reunited with the hard wooden slats of the playpen. The cold linoleum floor infuriates me. I feel like Cinderella after the ball, when the carriage has turned back into a pumpkin and the drivers are once again just mice.

Children in Erik's room sit on the floor, staring passively at nothing. The rug has literally been pulled out from under them.

I now feel awkward presenting the bag I'm carrying with toys and clothing purchased from the town department store to the caregivers in S-11, but I do it anyway. I have faith that some of the items may somehow make their way into the hands of the children who need them.

Erik is gloomy. He's teething, and can likely read the worry etched on my face. It's hailing outside, and the hallways seem darker and more foreboding than usual. As we walk the inner corridors of the children's home, I try to calm Erik with Latvian Christmas carols, carrying him and resting his head on my shoulder. After a long while, he becomes placid. Albert finds a couch for us to occupy on the second floor of the building. We take turns holding our son and read him the book about farm animals.

Erik points to the photos and rubs his tiny hand against the smiling lamb's coat. "Meh! Meh!"

Late in the afternoon at the Svoboda, despite the enormous lunch we enjoyed, John and Mary propose another evening out at the Palace hotel to clear our heads and improve our mood. We agree to meet in the hotel lobby at 19:30 sharp.

My husband and I are too tired to change clothes for dinner. We go upstairs to our room for a rest. Shortly before it's time to leave, we get up. I comb my hair, reapply some lipstick, and head to the door. Albert puts the key in the lock. It doesn't move at all, not to the right or left. He fidgets with it, carefully pushing, pulling, and twisting every way possible.

The key finally pops out, but we're locked inside. I head to the phone to call the reception desk. The line is dead.

Albert sits down and turns on the TV to watch an English language news broadcast on *Die Welt*.

"Someone will find us eventually," he shrugs.

Twenty minutes later, Mary and John are banging on our door.

"Hey, you guys in there?" John's voice is loud.

"Yeah. We can't get out," Albert shouts. He walks to the door. "Can I pass you my key over the hotel balcony, and could you try and open our door from the outside?"

"Sure. No problem." John sounds confident.

Given the wide gap between the two balconies, it's hard to say whether the key can successfully be passed. But since Albert and John have agreed to try, Mary and I pose no objections to the plan.

I hold my husband's legs with all my physical strength as he leans as far as he can through the space between the two balconies to try and reach John's fingers, which are stretching towards Albert's from the balcony next door. I consider that one of the men might drop the key, or slip out of their wife's grip and fall down three flights themselves onto the pavement below. Bam. Luckily, my man is cool as a cucumber, and John is too.

Fairly quickly, my husband is able to deliver the key to John. Both men go back safely into their rooms, and our neighbours manage to open the door to our guest room from the outside.

"Tonight, instead of one vodka, I'll have to order two," Albert remarks as the four of us exit the Svoboda on the way to the edge of the hill leading down toward the Palace.

Walking to dinner, I consider the fact that my husband could have passed the key to John and Mary more safely, if we'd all just thought about it for a moment. Albert could have thrown the key from our balcony onto our compatriots', or dropped our room key from the balcony straight down to the hotel's front pavement. Mary or John could have collected the key in either of these scenarios and opened our door. However, given that we are all singularly focused on completing the necessary steps to finalize the adoption of our children, we are not necessarily thinking clearly about anything else.

Our beloved Palace restaurant server, Anatoly, is once again flattering and gracious. He kindly asks for patience and explains the kitchen staff will need some extra time to prepare our dinner orders. No one is concerned, but Albert and John clearly need to "let loose." Mary and I watch them each order and down a few vodka shots and some beer. We join the men in consuming a beer or two with dinner.

Once everyone has calmed down from the day and loosened up, the conversation inevitably turns to our children.

Mary and John have jobs that require an international lifestyle. I imagine their children will experience diverse geographic locations, cultures, and ways of life. The couple's eyes light up when they talk about how they will soon legally be a family of four. With their thoughtful and measured personalities, I instinctively know Mary and John will be excellent parents to their kids.

Albert, meanwhile, can't wait to reconnect with his three daughters in Canada. "They're busy with school, friends, and community activities, but I like hearing what's new," my husband gushes. "I love the routine of helping with homework, driving my girls wherever they need to go, and just being at home sharing meals with them. It's a wonderful feeling."

I think back on our weeknight dinners at home with the girls. They're always buzzing with energy after a meal and love to joke and wrestle with Albert in the kitchen. It's fun to watch, especially because the girls are three against one, and Albert adores the attention.

I consider at this moment whether my husband always looks incredibly content and grounded because it's who he is, or if the experience of being a father to three ebullient daughters has made him so. He is among the most selfless and decent people I have ever met. I have no doubt that as Albert and I raise Erik together, our family bonds will grow even stronger.

Thoughts about child-rearing take me back to my own childhood. My brother, cousins, and I spent every summer at my family's cottage in Wasaga Beach, northwest of Toronto. We were four children running unfettered through vast green spaces for hours at a time. We played made-up games, hide-and-go-seek, and badminton, built sandcastles on the beach, and swam for hours each day in cold Georgian Bay.

My aunt, the only adult overseeing us, allowed our group to hike and bike on our own. On weekends when my parents and uncle arrived from the city, we performed elaborate plays for the adults in home-made costumes, devoured fresh cherries and peaches brought from Toronto, and learned how to cook hamburgers on a charcoal grill.

I want this for my son: freedom to explore, to be surrounded by nature, to let imagination run wild, to be self-reliant, and to become whatever he wants to be when he grows up.

******

The walk back up the hill to the Svoboda is treacherous. John and Albert stumble around, arm in arm, bragging about how brilliant they are. I can't see a thing in the dark, as John doesn't have his flashlight with him. I'm worried one of us will actually disappear down a deep pothole and never be seen again. Thankfully, Mary and I hold hands and we're relatively sober. We steer the gents upwards, pushing their backs and guiding them to move in the right direction. When the light from the Svoboda hotel streams onto the top of the hill, I'm grateful.

I request our guest room key from my husband upon our arrival at the third-floor landing of the hotel. There's no way he could wrestle the persnickety lock and key in his current state. Albert is happy to have me try. While initially employing a gentle approach to opening the door, I'm reminded that the lock and key are not anywhere near an ideal match. I change tactics to randomly push, pull, twist, jangle and rattle the key every which way. After a time, the door unlocks.

Albert clicks on the TV in our guest room but then quickly removes his clothes and climbs into bed. I find my pajamas and change into them.

I leave the TV on, but my mind is elsewhere.

Completing the paperwork for the adoption is an administrative quagmire. There's a long wait for each step to be completed and layers of documents to address. It's difficult to watch our son from a distance every day, living in the controlled conditions of an institution he is not allowed to leave.

My husband and I are stuck on the outside of the grounds looking in. When exactly will we be able to exit the children's home together with our son and fly to Canada?

Yolochka is run like an old Soviet style hospital where staff move around stone-faced in well-worn white lab coats. Children are kept quiet and mostly indoors, with little attention being paid to them as individual human beings. It's understandably not the caregivers' fault that the home can't provide what I consider to be the basic necessities of a child's life.

Ukraine has only been free of Russia for nine years. Seventy years of social, cultural and economic impoverishment under Soviet rule cannot be erased in such a short time. Coming from Canada, I have no right to pass judgement on how another country conducts its business, yet it's hard to swallow.

I wake my husband up in the middle of the night.

"What the hell are you doing?" he angrily blurts out. The stench of liquor on his breath is putrid.

"When we go to court in Simferopol next week, and the judge asks us if Erik has received medical clearance from Canada, what are we going to tell him? We won't have his papers by then."

"We'll talk about it in the morning. Goodnight."

"I can't sleep."

"I can."

"I'm phoning Laryssa Hrehoriv in Canada."

"What?"

"I'm calling now. Toronto time is about ten hours behind ours so she would still be awake."

"Why?"

"I need to check something."

In the middle of the night, when most people are sleeping, the phone in our guest room is in good working order. Of course!

Laryssa is surprised to hear from me so soon after the previous phone call. With prodding, she confirms that while she strictly advises us to have Canada's medical approval confirmed for Erik before going to court for a hearing, it's not a legal requirement from Ukraine's point of view. Ukraine doesn't care if Albert and I run into snags with Canada. Once Erik legally becomes our child, it's up to us to get him home.

"You're absolutely certain the boy will be approved by Canada?" I sense hesitation in Laryssa's voice.

"Yes. Erik is healthy, I'm sure of it. We have no intention of returning to Canada without him. By the time we get everything sorted in Simferopol, the doctor in Vienna should have had plenty of opportunity to put his stamp of approval on the file."

"The decision is ultimately up to you. My best advice is to be patient and proceed with caution. Let's stay in touch through email."

"Of course. Thank you for your help. Goodbye for now."

Albert is snoring loudly when I return to bed.

Smack on the Head

On a brisk December day, Albert and I are on our way to visit our son at the children's home for the last time before legally becoming his parents. We're trying to teach Yevgeny some simple phrases in English to pass time on the journey.

"*Hallo.*" He tries to get the greeting right but is still heavy on the "h" sounds. "*Wot eez yoor nehm? Weer can I drihv yooh?*"

"Very good, Yevgeny," I respond. "Thank you for the ride. See you later."

"*I seeh yooh.*"

"*Da. Spasibo,*" Albert confidently states.

I spring out of the car in the Yolochka driveway. The resident cats meander near the building's main entrance.

My husband carefully opens the heavy main metal door, but I forget to hold on to it as I follow him inside; the door slams loudly behind us when we enter the foyer. The elderly reception clerk raises her finger, but upon seeing the hopeful expression on my face, decides not to scold us.

I want to embrace the day and try to not worry too much. By the time the sun sets, I believe Albert and I will be the legal parents of our son, Erik.

The clerk studies my face to try and decipher what's going on. I'm grinning from ear to ear as I motion for permission for my husband and I to enter the inner area of the children's home. The lady can see something hopeful is in the air. She sweeps her arm high as she waves us through.

Erik stands up from a small wooden chair in his living space and runs straight for my husband when we appear in the doorway. Albert positions Erik on the shelf above the cubbyholes. We both kiss him on the cheek, and prepare to take him outdoors. Although we'll have a ten-day waiting period to endure before we can return to Kyiv with Erik, it doesn't seem so long anymore.

We haven't had any news from the Canadian doctor in Vienna about our son's medical file, but I refuse to let it bother me. "All in good time; stay positive," I say to myself.

Erik is now perfectly comfortable wearing the snowsuit we brought him from Canada, along with his sturdy new Turkish boots and the navy scarf, hat, and mitten set we purchased for him in the Simferopol department store. He's a stylish international dresser.

Although we've brought a carriage along, Erik declines to sit in the buggy and walks confidently beside it, holding my hand and my husband's as we stroll to the woods.

Our son will soon meet his whole family in Canada, some of his extended American family members, and many friends and other people who helped our family with the adoption. What an incredible moment of fulfillment and gratitude that will be.

The sun is bright in the sky and the forest has a soft glow. The day is perfect; the air feels electric.

After Erik consumes his snack, the three of us run around like crazed idiots in our forest playground. We jump up and down, howl like dogs, and purposely fall to the ground, kicking our feet in the air. Father and son joust, smacking sticks together hard, and Albert chases our son through brambly forest trails. Erik screeches and shouts out his wonderful sounds, expressing glee.

"Ooorh! Ah! Ah! Dhizz!"

Albert makes silly faces and sticks out his tongue. Erik and I laugh heartily.

Yevgeny is hovering around his car, looking solemn as Albert and I arrive a few minutes late for the drive back to the hotel. Tapping his wristwatch, the driver motions for us to hurry inside.

My husband is apologetic. "Did we mess up? Sorry, we didn't realize we were so late."

"At this point we're caught between reckless abandon and losing our minds with worry, so our brains have become scrambled eggs," I blurt out nonsensically.

The chauffeur doesn't waste any time driving; he's racing through the city to arrive at the Svoboda hotel in record time. Albert gestures for him to wait for us. The chauffeur lets us know with a shake of the head, a raise of the hand, and some sharp words in Russian that he is well aware he needs to wait for us.

We hurriedly dress for the court hearing. I nervously play with the gold cross on my necklace during the drive to the courthouse.

The car feels warm; I open the window for some fresh air. I finger my wedding ring, thinking back to my wedding day and relishing the fact that adopting Erik is a remarkable new milestone in our lives. He's already changed everything forever.

Iryna and Sofia circle Yevgeny's sedan upon our arrival near the courthouse. Sofia knocks on the window and motions for us to step out.

"Iryna will take you to designated hall for proceedings. I will be with John and Mary. Please hurry, and good luck."

My husband and I follow Iryna to the landing of the large stone building. We snap a few photos before entering.

Inside, we race upstairs to the courtroom. Along the way, we pass by several intimidating halls of justice where prisoners are seated gloomily in black wrought iron cages, watching the proceedings. I don't know if this type of cage is standard around the world. Not having ever entered a Canadian courtroom, I have no idea if such cages exist in our homeland.

Thankfully, the stately courtroom where our case will be heard does not appear to have a prisoner's cage. It reminds me of American TV show courtrooms. I relax a bit. Judge Judy, are you here in the building somewhere? I could use some zany American humour at this moment.

Judge Yurkovich sits self-assuredly in a black robe and ceremonial sash behind a voluminous, raised bench. A gavel rests by his right hand. To the left of the judge is a young blonde woman tapping away on a keyboard on a tiny table, whom I take to be the court reporter. Ukrainian flags and other insignia are displayed near the bench.

Judge Yurkovich notes in his introductory remarks that Mr. S.V. Ivanov, the young prosecutor from Kyiv, seated directly across from us, will participate in the court hearing. The man's angular face and pointy nose remind me of a mouse. He's the guy we saw at the children's home; now I know for sure who the prosecutor is, but the fact that he visited Yolochka when we were forced to make ourselves scarce is disquieting.

Iryna is directed to a chair positioned slightly behind and just to the right of my husband. The judge acknowledges that she will provide verbal translation of the proceedings into English.

While the judge's demeanor is solemn but not in any way menacing, the prosecutor tries to deliberately unsettle Albert and I. He taps a pen in his hand and gives us the death stare.

For a moment, I panic and become confused. What is the prosecutor doing in our court hearing? Through Iryna, we learn that Mr. Ivanov has asked to participate in some hearings in Simferopol and to ascertain which particular adoptions will be allowed to proceed. Really? Does that mean some may be denied?

I feel my cheeks turn red but force myself to remain outwardly unruffled. If ever there was a time to project serenity, confidence, and composure, this is it. My legs are trembling under my skirt and my heart is racing, but I stare expressionless back at the prosecutor, letting him know we have nothing to hide and won't be intimidated.

My husband and I are told by the judge not to speak unless spoken to. Seated side by side, we hold hands and try hard to look straight ahead. Both of us have wet palms.

Judge Yurkovich repeats the questions we've already answered numerous times about why we are planning to adopt a child from Ukraine. For example, do we have the means to raise him, what is our motivation for adopting Erik specifically, and are we aware of his medical status?

Albert cogently responds to the questions about our financial status and motivation for adoption. My husband and I have learned during the course of our trip that whatever I say in a formal setting in Ukraine could be seen to hold less weight than what my husband would impart, based on my gender.

My husband and I briefly make eye contact in response to the medical question. I conjecture that the judge may be referring to the hydrocephalus diagnosis in Erik's medical file, which Dr. Bohdan assured us was made in error. After a brief moment, Albert responds "yes" loudly to the question about our awareness of the health status of the child.

"It is our hope that you will grant us legal standing as parents of this child. It is our conviction that we are ready and able to adopt him based on the information we have been provided and the medical assessment of the physician," my husband adds. Judge Yurkovich probes no further.

The hearing lasts about three quarters of an hour. In between the judge's questions, the prosecutor scribbles on a notepad. He rises for a moment to ask Albert if we have been coerced in any way, if we have any knowledge of procedures that aren't being followed, and why we have chosen a child from the Simferopol orphanage in particular.

Albert answers decisively. "We do not see that the adoption authorities we have encountered in Ukraine have done anything wrong, nor have we done anything wrong. The National Adoption Centre in Kyiv invited us to visit the child they identified for us in Simferopol. We agreed. We did not choose on our own to come to Simferopol; it's where we were directed to go by your own authorities in Kyiv."

Mr. Ivanov sits back down, writes something, and lets the judge know he's done.

Judge Yurkovich's final question rattles my husband. He asks Albert to state the day, month, and year of our wedding. My husband looks stunned, unable to respond. He seems to be calculating the date in his head. I nudge him in the side and try to get him to look inside his wedding ring, as our wedding date is engraved in each of our rings. The judge chastises me for gesturing to my husband. Albert regains his composure and answers correctly.

Once the hearing is completed, we are escorted by the judge's assistant to a low bench just outside the courtroom and told to wait. The bench is narrow and stiff, but I don't mind. It's a better option than standing against a wall or waiting outside in the cold.

As I install myself on the bench, my body shivers, and I suddenly feel very cold. I close my eyes and try to calm down, as I'm wrestling with nervous excitement and exhaustion. I realize I'm having an anxiety attack, which I haven't had in a long time. Given that Albert and I are in the midst of a monumentally significant day, it's not surprising that I need to intentionally quiet my mind. It's only a matter of time before we'll be asked back inside the courtroom to learn the outcome of the hearing, so I'll need to pull myself together before then.

Albert removes his suit jacket and loosens his tie. I touch his back and can feel his shirt is drenched. I take his hand for a moment. While mine is ice cold, his is raging hot. I'm beat from the drama of the courtroom but eager to receive the judgment of the court. I look at my husband; he's beaming. It went well, he's silently telling me.

I breathe in and out slowly several times, and gradually feel my body losing some of the out-of-control feeling. After a few minutes, the anxiety wanes.

I remove my high-heeled shoes and stretch my feet straight out, circle my ankles and move my feet up and down. I'd like to stand up and jump a bit to warm up, but decide against doing that in such an official setting.

The prosecutor exits the courtroom and strides impassively past us, swinging his arms at his sides without acknowledging our presence.

I'm afraid to speak, wondering if the court rules prohibit dialogue. The building is eerily quiet, apart from doors slamming every now and then and people's feet creaking on the wooden flooring as they walk by. Iryna is reviewing a document as she slowly saunters towards us from the judge's chambers, her red cape draping her body.

"The hearing is concluded. All documentation has been approved as correct. The decision will be provided later today."

Iryna implores us not to leave the bench for any reason. She excuses herself, indicating she'll return within two hours to wait alongside us for the decision.

Time passes surprisingly quickly. People occasionally move through the hallway, mumbling in hushed voices or studying documents. An old man taps the hallway floor hard with a cane as he takes each step, as if in pain. He's deeply hunched over yet holding his head up as much as possible. His tattered suit jacket and dirty work boots have seen better days.

Eventually, the judge's assistant emerges in the hallway and motions for us to return to the courtroom. We stand up and follow her, believing Iryna is already in the courtroom.

Judge Yurkovich is slightly annoyed when he realizes our translator is not present, but we are nonetheless shown to our chairs. He begins conversing with us in English, revealing that he spent time studying in America. He grabs a family photo album from atop the bench, climbs down, and brings it over to our seats to show us. There are photos of the judge's family, as well as some from his time in the USA. We reciprocate by sharing our family photo album with him, making small talk with Judge Yurkovich while awaiting Iryna's arrival. He asks about the harshness of Canadian winters and praises the brawn of Canada's hockey players. During his time in the United States, he watched National Hockey League games on television. He expresses admiration for Canadian players' skill and expertise in leading the sport globally.

"I sincerely apologize," Iryna declares as she rushes into the room, her red cape flapping behind. She exchanges a few brief words with Judge Yurkovich and takes her seat. The judge clambers back atop his bench.

The court reporter readies herself for the decision. Judge Yurkovich reads the decree in Ukrainian, with Iryna translating. It takes about fifteen minutes to deliver. I'm so wound up the only words I can retain include my name, my husband's, our son's, Yolochka, Simferopol, Crimea, and Yalta, which are all referenced.

The reporter stops typing. Judge Yurkovich descends from his bench and extends a hand to Albert.

"Congratulations."

The judge shakes my hand, as well. I don't know if it's appropriate to speak, so I remain silent.

Once the court reporter leaves the room, the judge's assistant comes in, smiling. I spontaneously hug her and break down crying. The assistant's eyes also fill with tears. She hugs me back, assuring me all is well.

Judge Yurkovich tells us to wait. With the formal session completed, the printed decree will arrive momentarily.

"*Dyakuyu*. Thank you!" I say.

The assistant returns shortly with the printed document. Albert hands it to Iryna so she can translate it into English.

On the way down the stairs of the courthouse, Iryna whispers that we are now officially the parents of a lovely boy, and she congratulates us. Albert asks about the ten-day waiting period and when it will end.

The translator explains that because it's now late on a Friday afternoon, we won't be able to get the decree notarized and confirmed in the court records until Monday. So, the waiting period for our adoption will officially be over in thirteen days. After that, we have the right to remove Erik from the children's home and fly to Kyiv to complete the last remaining steps of the adoption.

As Yevgeny pulls the car away from the courthouse, Albert and I are buoyant. I want to kiss my son, hold him, and tell him that mom and dad will soon be taking him home to Canada.

"Yolochka!" I shout from the back of the car.

Iryna turns and looks awkwardly back at us from the front seat.

"I am sorry; visitation at the children's home is over for today."

"What do you mean? Erik is now legally our son," Albert says. "We're his parents. We have rights."

"Ah, yes," Iryna concurs. "But you must understand, the situation remains the same with the children's home. Visitation hours are to be respected, rules are in place regarding food, and so on."

"But we're the legal guardians."

"Albert and Sandra, after thirteen days you will have your son. Until then, please respect the procedures."

Sofia is cradling a large bottle of champagne and dangling several champagne flutes between her fingers when we enter our hotel. The clerks behind the reception desk applaud us.

Mary and John are seated on a low couch in the foyer in their smart business suits, looking as though they've already downed some bubbly, their cheeks red and lips spread wide, exposing toothy smiles. They, too, went to court today and emerged victorious.

"Please join us," Sofia coos, with a wide smile. Her floral perfume is pleasant. She pours a generous amount of pink champagne into the glasses; we raise our flutes in a toast.

"Congratulations to wonderful parents and children. It is honour to help two nice families."

John counters with a toast of his own. "To Sofia and Iryna, the marvelous ladies who help create families. We sincerely thank you."

Albert is grinning broadly. "Sofia and Iryna, your diligent efforts on our behalf are tremendously appreciated."

The glasses clink loudly together. I down a huge gulp. The beverage is refreshing and slightly sweet. Albert and John joke that we'll need to consume the entire bottle right then and there to release the stress and drama of the court hearings.

The significance of the day is beginning to hit me. I'm now legally Erik's mom, and Albert, his dad. I'm crazy happy! My heart is bursting with love for my son, and for my husband who is sharing the adventure.

As it's Friday night, the hotel reception area is getting busy with arriving guests.

Sipping champagne from our corner of the lobby, we watch groups of people check in with their luggage and we play a game of guessing where they're from.

A slight, middle-aged man in a black suit appears in the foyer. Beside him is a young woman in red high heels wearing an elegant fur coat. The man looks pleased with his companion. He strokes her face, and winks at her.

"I have no idea where they're from, but I can guess what their plans might be," John chuckles.

"To making plans," Albert says, clinking his glass against mine.

Once the man and woman have left the lobby and headed upstairs, three burly men with muddy boots, ripped pants, and flannel shirts stumble in through the entrance.

Mary and I simultaneously yell out, "Construction workers!"

A stench of alcohol fills the lobby; the gents have apparently been drinking heavily. The trio goads the front desk staff, shouting what appear to be obscenities. One of them picks up a stack of brochures on the counter, and tosses them to the floor.

The clerks are annoyed. The older one shows the trio outside with her arm pointing to the main door, but the men don't budge. One of them grabs a pen off the counter, and stuffs it into his pocket. He lights a cigarette. Another leans against the lobby wall and argues with the third companion. They raise their voices, and one of the three, nearly bald, pushes the other. The third man laughs. The older hotel worker raises her voice to the group. They ignore her.

Soon, two of the men are punching each other hard with their fists and exchanging cross words. The third enjoys the show, laughing from the sidelines. Finally, the two inebriated fighting men stagger to the stairs, go up a few steps and start to turn left, toward the small cafe. But the bald one suddenly trips and falls, smashing his head on the main stone stairs. The other man crumples down on top of him. Blood gushes out of the injured man's head; the other two men start yelling.

Sofia declares the celebration is concluded. We down our champagne glasses and agree to meet later in the lobby to proceed to the Palace hotel for dinner.

Albert and I quickly step around the two men on the stairs and dash up to the third floor, seeking to avoid any contact with the rowdy trio. Mary and John are directly behind us, with Sofia and Iryna following.

Safe on our guest room balcony, we watch for the arrival of an ambulance. After a long time, we give up and head back inside.

"Maybe the ambulance goes to a side entrance or something," Albert speculates, scratching his head as he closes the balcony door.

"I didn't hear any sirens."

"Maybe they don't use sirens here."

We remove our business attire and collapse into bed for a short nap.

Later, on the way down to the lobby, I see blood stains smeared along the walls of the stairwell and blood on the steps. A woman is scrubbing the floor in the hotel reception area. We don't dare ask about the brawl or what's happened to the men.

Dinner at the Palace is once again memorable. Despite John's earlier advice about avoiding the region's wine, Albert orders a bottle of sparkling white wine, feeling the occasion demands a statement. The Georgian wine is light with a hint of sweetness. The bottle is quickly emptied.

The meal tastes wonderful, because it could not be otherwise. I savour the stewed meats, spiced cabbage, and pancakes stuffed with meat and vegetables on my plate as if I had not eaten for days. Iryna orders extra toppings on her ice cream and manages to consume the entire bowl.

Anatoly is more than pleased to accommodate our requests. He congratulates us on the successful outcomes of our court proceedings and offers a complimentary round of cognacs for the group. We accept the gesture and leave a hefty tip.

By the end of the evening, everyone at our table is subdued. Sofia and Iryna, while visibly pleased with themselves and the gargantuan feat they have accomplished on our behalf, look fatigued. Scanning the table, I note that we all have puffy eyes and slightly messy hair. The battle wounds are showing.

The next morning at the Svoboda, there's no sign of the previous evening's melee. The stairway walls and stairs have been cleaned. My husband and I head out the door for breakfast.

A mid-size transport truck is idling in the parking lot near the front entrance. Someone is yelling out the passenger side window. I recognize the face as one of the three rambunctious men from the previous evening. He isn't the one who was injured.

I stand on the pavement for a moment staring at the truck. A man almost knocks me over from the side as he rushes by me. It's the guy with the smashed head. His face is a sickly shade of white-green; the fellow looks barely alive. The massive gash on the side of his bald head is horrific; dried blood has coagulated around the deep wound, which does not seem to have been attended to. The man climbs up into the driver's side of the truck and takes the wheel. He hits the gas, and slowly maneuvers the truck out of the parking lot.

******

After weeks of running around in Simferopol trying to complete Erik's adoption, it appears our last days in Crimea will not be as tranquil as I'd hoped they might be.

The Canadian physician in Vienna in charge of approving our son's medical file continues to stall. Back from vacation, the doctor hasn't confirmed Erik's good health. We learn from the Embassy of Canada in Kyiv that medical clearance is usually completed within two working days when a child is deemed healthy. We've been waiting more than two weeks.

Despite the advice of Laryssa Hrehoriv, our Toronto adoption agent, to leave the process to local fixers and not get pushy ourselves because that won't help in Ukraine, my husband and I decide to take matters into our own hands. After all, it's not Ukraine that is stalling our son's medical file; it's Canada.

Prior to leaving Canada, we connected with Dennis Mills, the federal member of parliament representing our local Toronto area riding at the national level. Given his constituency office is only a few blocks away from our Toronto home, we dropped in to see Mr. Mills before leaving for Ukraine. We explained about our international adoption plans and asked if we could contact him should any problems arise while we're in Ukraine completing the adoption. Mr. Mills kindly affirmed he would help in any way possible.

We also contacted Sarmite (Sam) Bulte, the only Canadian member of parliament of Latvian origin, whom Albert and I are acquainted with, to see if she would help if needed. Sarmite agreed. So, given the current conundrum with the Vienna doctor, we sent emails to both members of parliament asking them to inquire with the Vienna doctor on our behalf.

Mid-December is fast approaching. Albert and I are concerned the physician might soon disappear for an end-of-year break. Without Canadian medical clearance, we can't finalize Erik's landed immigrant status with Canada, nor obtain his visa to enter the country.

Within two days of receiving our emails, both members of Canada's parliament fax letters to the Embassy of Canada in Kyiv and to Vienna, asking if there is a way to complete the recommendation on Erik's file expeditiously. They both email us copies of the letters they'd sent.

Simultaneous to all of this, Laryssa is making inquiries with Canadian government officials in Ottawa on our behalf.

And, just in case it's required, I connect with a public relations colleague of mine in Ottawa named Genevieve Blanchette. Genevieve promises to "rain hell" on the Canadian government through a national media relations campaign should our son's medical clearance continue to stall. The campaign would pose the question of why Canada is dithering and potentially keeping a family apart at Christmas. Genevieve is on standby, ready to pounce if needed.

All we can do now is wait.

"Hopefully we'll hear some positive news soon," Albert tells me.

Yalta

Nineteenth century Russian writer Anton Chekhov spent much of the last five years of his life in Yalta due to failing health from tuberculosis. No longer able to endure the harsh Moscow winters, Chekov preferred the warm and healing air on the Black Sea coast.

Ensconced in the White Dacha, a Yalta villa he'd built for himself, the writer produced some of his most acclaimed plays, including *Three Sisters* and *The Cherry Orchard*.

It is to Yalta, early one morning, that my husband and I are traveling to address an important step in our son's adoption. Chekhov's final play, *The Cherry Orchard*, sticks in my mind as we near the subtropical city with Iryna and Yevgeny. In the play, an aristocratic landowner returns to her family estate as it is about to be auctioned for the mortgage. The owner, Madame Ranevskaya, refuses an offer to lease out some of her land and the family loses their property.

Following a long period of internal stagnation, growing unrest, and a political crisis that resulted in the Soviet parliament voting to end itself, the dissolution of the Soviet Union in 1991 presents an interesting parallel to turn-of-the-century Russia, which could not ultimately find a viable way forward.

With Russia losing control of the European countries it had occupied since World War Two and Vladimir Putin installed as president, the country has veered from the democratic path it started on and reverted to an autocracy. I wonder what the future holds.

"Hey, look at all the palm trees," Albert notes as he rolls down the car window to feel the balmy air, taking me out of my reflections.

Located on the site of an ancient colony founded by Greek settlers in the first century who were looking for a safe shore, Yalta was originally given the name *Yalos* (shore). In the late eighteenth century, Crimean Tatars who inhabited the area started leaving the peninsula when the Russian empire captured the region.

While the city is now known for health tourism and beach vacations, it also possesses rich historic and cultural treasures and a vibrant night life.

Yalta is our son's birth place. We are in the city to engage with officials at the birth registry office and to update Erik's birth certificate with his legal name so he can acquire a Ukrainian passport in preparation to leave for Canada.

Yevgeny brings his car to a stop in front of an historic gray and white stone building. Iryna instructs my husband and I to get out. Yevgeny and Iryna have a short verbal exchange before she steps out of the car to join us; Yevgeny slowly pulls his car away.

Through light cloud cover, I can see the deep bay of the seashore in the distance and a surrounding mountain range.

Behind us is a walking promenade framed by palm trees. The breeze in the air is fragrantly scented with pine and the sea. The bird sounds remind me of seagulls frolicking along Wasaga Beach back home in Canada. The softly crashing waves provide a calming echo of my childhood.

Iryna is eager to process the birth certificate, as we intend to return to Simferopol at the end of the day. While it's only 8:30 and our appointment is for 9:00, there's already a queue of people in the hallway on the ground floor waiting to get in to the registry office. Albert and I take our positions at the back of the line while Iryna strides to the front to see what she can possibly do to move things along expeditiously.

At 9:30, by some miracle of Iryna's making, we're invited to enter the birth registry director's bureau. Large arched windows face a treed garden. A smartly dressed woman stands by her desk. Pleasantries and handshakes are exchanged with Iryna before the lady sets down on a wooden swivel chair behind her desk. The director is poised and seems pleasant. Taking a number of documents from Iryna, including our passports, I note the woman's manicured nails have bubble gum pink nail polish. A diamond-encrusted ring is prominent on her long slender ring finger.

We wait a few moments while the director reviews the materials.

"Oh, what is this?" the lady queries.

Iryna quietly moves directly beside the director's desk and studies what she is referring to.

"Please, Albert and Sandra, can you take a rest?"

My husband and I retreat to two chairs against the far wall across from the director's workspace. We look at each other straight-faced; my husband shrugs and pulls his *Cold Mountain* novel out of his backpack. I reach into my handbag to retrieve my notebook and pen.

"Here we go again; this could take a while," we express to each other with our eyes.

The banter between Iryna and the director involves repeated use of what appears to be the word, "Canada." A string of additional comments follows, along with physical pointing to various parts of printed documents which Iryna has provided, including our passports. Iryna is explaining something, but the lady doesn't look happy.

The Yalta functionary politely says, "No." Iryna looks exasperated but stands firm.

I try to focus on my notepad and compose some thoughts but end up scribbling circles and triangles all over the page. We've hit another roadblock.

About half an hour passes before there is a lull in the conversation. Iryna straightens her back and we make eye contact. She invites us to get up and follow the two ladies into another room down the hall.

In the second, smaller room, the director articulates a few sentences to a man behind a desk and gestures for him to look at Albert. He does. She shows the man several documents, including our passports, and exchanges words with Iryna. After a moment, the lady shakes Iryna's hand and we are ushered out of the room.

As we make our way through the building to the front exit, Iryna shares good news.

"The birth certificate will be ready in about two hours."

"Great!" Albert is pleased.

Outside in the courtyard, the translator recounts the slight hiccup. "The outside of your passports is clearly marked 'Canada,'" Iryna begins. "However, inside it says your nationality is 'Canadian.' The director was expecting the nationality to be 'Canada.' It took some time to convince her to accept 'Canadian.' I presented to her the document stating that in Judge Yurkovich's court decree he also identifies your nationality as 'Canadian,' but the director needed convincing that it could be used on your son's birth certificate. In addition, she was displeased that Erik is not taking Albert's first name—the patronym, as his second name. She did in the end acquiesce, but it was nonetheless a difficult conversation."

I have much to learn from Iryna's unruffled, patient, and tactful approach. Had I been negotiating with the birth registry officer things may not have ended as successfully for us.

Iryna makes a quick mobile call to Yevgeny, who arrives momentarily to drive us to a local bank, where we pre-pay for the birth certificate.

We have some free time while the birth certificate is being produced. Iryna, Albert, and I take a leisurely walk past small cafes, souvenir shops, and restaurants, stopping at a cafe with a big soda pop graphic sign hanging outside. I go inside to purchase three small bottles of mango juice for our group. We sit at a wrought iron table in front of the cafe while consuming the beverages. The palm trees and flowering bushes adorning the street are a beautiful accent to the picturesque surroundings.

Further in the city there's a bustling outdoor market where vendors display assorted household items and a variety of fresh produce, including onions, leeks, hanging garlic strings, potatoes, tomatoes, grapes and pears. All of the produce looks fresh and robust, as it's grown in the area's warm, moist climate. I buy some grapes for our group to share on the ride back to Simferopol.

Heading back to the birth registry office, we purposely walk beyond the building and go all the way to the water's edge to take a look. Albert and I collect a few small rocks from the shoreline, mementos from the Black Sea for our son.

The three of us return to the birth registry office at the agreed-upon time, where Iryna carefully reviews Erik's new document. She notices the certificate is missing a stamp, indicating it is a copy, and not the original.

The original should remain in the birth registry's archives, Iryna insists. The clerk declines Iryna's request for the stamp, telling her this is no longer a requirement. Our translator refuses to budge and ignores the request to leave the office. Albert and I are made to wait in the hallway while the issue is sorted out. The door quietly closes behind us.

"I thought it was too good to be true," Albert admits, "that we could finalize the birth certificate so quickly. What else will they ask us to do? Handstands for the director?"

After a few moments, the director passes us in the hallway and heads straight into the bureau where Iryna is negotiating on our behalf.

I break out laughing. "Here it comes, honey, they are literally going to ask you to do handstands. How strong are your upper body muscles?"

Albert grins. "Super strong!"

About three quarters of an hour later, Iryna emerges victorious from the registry clerk's office.

"Come, we must hurry." Iryna punches in Yevgeny's cell phone number on the way out the door.

"What happened?"

"It was problematic. They would not agree to my request. I had to telephone justice ministry in Kyiv to corroborate importance of the stamp, which they affirmed. I asked Yalta birth registry director to speak to Kyiv in person to verify the requirement. So now we have the stamp and we must hurry back to Simferopol. We will need to present the document to Justice Ministry there today."

"Today? It's already mid-afternoon."

"Let's try our best to make it. The timing is important."

On the way back to Simferopol I fall asleep in the car. I'm awakened by my husband poking me in the side.

"Hey, get up. We're at the Justice Ministry and we need to move quickly!"

I'm lethargic from the nap. Albert hurriedly pulls me by my hand up three flights of stairs to the Simferopol justice ministry, where we need to process an additional stamp on Erik's birth certificate.

Once imprinted, we race down to the second floor to pay for the stamp. Then we race back up to the third floor to get another stamp, and dash back down to the second floor yet again to make an additional payment. Then it's "hurry up and wait" in the hallway for the final "new" birth certificate, which we receive at exactly two minutes before the 17:00 closing time.

"Let's do this again tomorrow!" I joke to Iryna.

"Humour is occasionally appropriate in these moments," she replies, poker-faced.

Albert and I fall into the back seat of the car and start laughing; we can't stop for several minutes.

Later the same evening, there's a knock on our guest room door.

"Albert, Sandra, are you there?"

"Yes, Iryna. One minute, please. I need to fight with the lock here."

My husband tortuously jingles and jangles the key until it pops out of the mechanism and the door unlocks.

"Hi, what can we do for you?"

"May I step in to your room for a moment?"

"Of course. Please, come in."

"Thank you, Albert."

By the serious look on Iryna's face, I'm guessing something is wrong.

"Hi, Iryna, what's up?"

"Oh, please don't be alarmed. Here, this is for you. I just finished translating into English. I hope this will be of interest, and that you will keep this information for Erik, just in case. Now that the court case is completed and the court decree was in your favour, I thought you might want it."

Iryna hands my husband a document. I read it over his shoulder. It's a letter of consent for adoption from our son's birth mother, with some identifying information. The birth mother provides a statement:

"I do not object to placement of this child for adoption. I shall have no grudge against the adoptive parents. I have been informed of the legal consequences of placement of the child for adoption."

"Thank you, Iryna, we appreciate you providing this to us. It's very helpful. We will keep it safe. See you in the morning." My husband slowly closes and locks the door. "Well, if Erik ever wants to know, we can give this to him."

"It doesn't change anything. He's our son, and we love him."

"Of course. But if he ever wants to learn any more, we have some basic information."

Climbing in to bed, I'm reminded once again that the thirteen-day waiting period for our son is counting down.

"What if the Vienna doctor never approves Erik's medical file?" I blurt out, just as my husband is closing his eyes in bed.

"That's not going to happen."

"Then why don't we have it already?"

"I have no idea, but I'm bushed. Goodnight."

"Goodnight."

I toss and turn and can't sleep. After a while, I rouse my husband.

"Hey, wake up, I'm worried about the Vienna physician."

"Huh? What do you mean?"

"We've sent letters to two members of parliament. Laryssa is liaising with her Canadian government contacts. Svitlana is trying to help from Kyiv. I don't understand why the Vienna doctor won't finish the medical approval. It doesn't make sense!"

"He hasn't gotten around to finalizing Erik's file, that's all."

"Why? What's taking so long? What if something else is happening? What if one day we go to visit Erik and he's gone? What if he disappears from the children's home? Why else would the prosecutor visit? Have other children gone missing? I'll lose my mind if we can't bring Erik back to Canada with us."

"That won't happen. We're both exhausted. We need to sleep. Stop tormenting yourself. Everything will work out."

"We have no control over what is happening here. Our son is legally ours, but we can't spend any time with him anywhere in Simferopol except for the grounds of the children's home—that's completely nuts!"

"Stop worrying. You're tired from the Yalta trip. We'll be leaving soon for Canada and Erik will be with us when we go."

"Can you absolutely promise me that?"

"Yes. I promise."

******

Together with John and Mary, Albert and I ask Sofia to travel back to Kyiv to begin processing the final documents for our departure from Ukraine. This is intended to save time, as well as to spare us from having to run around Kyiv with our children in tow, waiting in line at the National Adoption Centre at the Ministry of Education and Science and visiting other government offices to complete some remaining papers.

Nearing the end of our adoption journey in Ukraine, Erik is becoming extremely attached to us, as we are to him. He laughs unabashedly during our daily play time in the woods and skips through the halls during indoor visits, holding our hands. He sings along in his own baby language to our Latvian Christmas carols. Our son is now visibly distraught each time we leave him. I'm crushed that we can't bring him to our hotel so that we can all be together, but I force a smile when we part so as not to upset him.

The last few days of playing with Erik in the forest are trying. My husband and I now frequently joke about running off with our son and hopping on the next plane to Kyiv. Albert misses his girls terribly. He's tried to communicate with emails nearly every day and is thrilled to receive any news of their lives in Toronto.

Surprisingly, the American election results remain unresolved. My husband and I joke that we'll be back in Canada before the vote recount is confirmed and Al Gore or George W. Bush is declared the winner.

Week Five

Leaving Simferopol

The day before our thirteen-day waiting period is over, Sofia calls our hotel guest room to say she's received a call informing her that the Vienna doctor has approved Erik's medical file. Our son is cleared to travel to Canada. Albert and I jump up and down on the bed in our guest room, nearly breaking it.

"Call off the media relations campaign," my husband says to me. "We won't need to get down and dirty after all."

"Got it. I'll email Genevieve as soon as we get to an internet cafe."

Mary and John have also completed their final papers and both of their children are cleared to leave Ukraine.

******

Celebrated Canadian poet Leonard Cohen has been quoted as saying, "This world is full of conflicts and full of things that

cannot be reconciled. But there are moments when we can … reconcile and embrace the whole mess, and that's what I mean by 'Hallelujah.'"

It is in the spirit of expression of Hallelujah, or gratitude, that my husband and I set out to leave a gesture of small gifts for people in Simferopol who played a pivotal role in helping us complete some critical steps in the adoption of our son, Erik.

The day before leaving the city for good, Albert and I make a final trip to the Simferopol courthouse. We have a bottle of Canadian whisky we've brought with us from Canada and a wrapped box of French perfume.

Yevgeny delivers us to the front door of the courthouse and Albert and I get out of the car. My husband and I scurry up the stairs to Judge Yurkovich's office.

Arriving at the antechamber to the office, we present his assistant with the perfume, and show her that the whisky bottle is intended for her boss. Judge Yurkovich happens to open the door to his chambers. He looks surprised to see us. Nervously, my husband hands him the bottle. The judge smiles and shakes our hands. I watch him quickly retreat back inside his office and lock the bottle away in a cabinet beside his desk. Judge Yurkovich bows his head to us; we understand it as a signal to leave.

Running down the stairs, we pass Mr. Ivanov, the young prosecutor from Kyiv, as he is heading upstairs. We smile uneasily at him, but the man ignores us. Albert and I then bolt out the door and jump into Yevgeny's car, laughing.

"Wow, that was close," my husband says. "We could have gotten ourselves into a sticky situation."

Our chauffeur speeds off to an apothecary, where we purchase an assortment of prescription medicines for children at Yolochka which the facility's head physician has requested. There is no fee for adopting a child from Ukraine, but donations to children's homes are welcome. Apart from securing the prescription drugs, we also deposit money into the institution's bank account that will be used to buy food for the children.

We arrive at the children's home for the afternoon visit. We have a bag with us filled with presents. I give the old lady in the reception area a toque and matching scarf, emblazoned with a red Canadian maple leaf motif.

The clerk places the toque proudly on her head, and kisses me on the cheek, holding my face in her hands for a moment. Gazing intently into her eyes, I see that the lady is letting me know not to worry, it's okay for Albert and I to take our son to Canada, to his new family. I nod my head, indicating that we'll take very good care of Erik. I hug the lady tightly, telling her, "*Spasibo*." We leave a bottle of Canadian whisky for the Yolochka director with his assistant.

Inside the living space of room S-11, Erik is aware something significant is happening. He discerns by the happy look on my face and my husband's that the end of his stay at Yolochka is nearing.

We present the caregivers in Erik's room with the remaining items in our bag: assorted Canadian cosmetics and boxes of chocolate. I gesture to the women with my hands that these are to be shared.

The woman who receives the bag from me on the caregivers' behalf provides a series of comments I wish I could understand; "*spasibo*" is sprinkled throughout the remarks.

"*Spasibo*," I say back to her. I bow my head to all of the caregivers, letting them know with my hand on my heart that we sincerely appreciate their efforts.

The last afternoon walk through the dark hallways of the children's home with our son is particularly trying. Our three plane tickets are booked. All of the adoption business in Simferopol is done. The Canadian doctor has verified Erik's good health and we're cleared to leave. A few days of preparing some final documents in Kyiv lie ahead, but the three of us will be together, and that's all that matters. I want to leave the children's home with my son that very minute. It feels cruel to have to wait one more day.

Erik brings me back to reality when he grabs my hand tightly, and my husband's, and allows us to swing him through our arms as we walk. He kicks his feet up high in front of us, lets his hands go, jumps forcefully and lands straight ahead. We repeat the move again and again, signaling how much we've bonded as a family, and I'm reminded how much stronger our son has grown since we first met him. Erik has waited a long time for a mom and dad to love him. In his own way, he encourages me that I can wait one more day for us to be together.

The sky is gloomy and overcast on our last night in Crimea. The damp air makes my bones ache, but my spirits aren't diminished. Preparing for our last hurrah at the Palace hotel with our group from the United States, Canada, and Kyiv feels like a New Year's Eve celebration. My husband and I dress up for the occasion and bring along our still photo camera so we can take some shots of our group and Anatoly, the server who has taken such good care of us during the past month.

John lights up the road ahead down the steep, foggy hill with his flashlight as we amble cautiously down toward the commercial street below leading to the Palace. We alerted Anatoly a couple of days earlier that this would be our last meal at the restaurant and asked that he please reserve our regular booth.

Iryna fidgets with the large scarf around her shoulders as we enter the hotel, stating she will be eating a full-course dinner, although no one believes her. The translator is buoyant about the prospect of reuniting with her husband after a long absence.

We step into the dining hall of the Palace and approach our usual booth. The table is set with gold-plated dinnerware, crystal stem-wear, and a white lace tablecloth overlay. A silver candelabrum with white burning candles illuminates the dark space. Mary and I wonder out loud if Anatoly has forgotten about us and is instead expecting important guests.

John points to a sign on the table. "It means the table is reserved."

"Please, be seated." Anatoly appears out of nowhere, straddling a bucket of chilled champagne.

What an incredibly kind gesture. What has the server to gain by presenting us with such a beautiful table? We won't be returning to dine in the establishment; he knows our departure is imminent.

Albert and John offer a special toast to Anatoly, who allows us to take some photos of him. The champagne is gone before the appetizers arrive. I feel giddy and don't care how I will stumble up the hill back to our hotel.

The last feast at the Palace is particularly decadent. Mouth-watering lobster and shrimp salad, succulent leg of lamb, heavenly garlic potatoes, and feathery light chocolate mousse crown a magical trip. It shocks me that with all the food I've consumed through our time in Ukraine I've lost thirteen kilos in body weight. All of my skirts and slacks are now loose and ill fitting. Albert has also lost weight, although neither of us is complaining. (There are side benefits to experiencing periods of extreme stress.)

Iryna describes the following day's itinerary while pushing food around on her plate. We'll have the morning visit with our children as usual and then return to the Svoboda to pack our bags and check out. We won't be permitted to return to Yolochka to retrieve our children until 15:00, as that is the time stated in documents the children's home director signed as the approved hour for the children's release. Our flight is due to leave at 16:30.

"Any way to move up the release time from the children's home by a bit?" John asks.

"No. It is not possible; 15:00 is the official time. Don't worry, we will make the trip."

Iryna shares that Yevgeny and Viktor want to make our afternoon wait as pleasant as possible by treating our group to cake and tea at their favorite Simferopol tearoom before heading to Yolochka.

"You will see," she tells us. "It will be a nice end to your stay in Crimea."

The evening is ending quietly when Anatoly arrives at our table with some books. He hands my husband a novel written by Latvian author Alberts Bels—an English translation of the writer's Latvian poems that a guest gave the server many years ago.

"Serendipity," Albert says, offering Anatoly a book he's just finished reading and has brought along as a gift to the server. "It's called *Cold Mountain*, a story about the American Civil War."

"Oh, thank you, an unexpected but welcome surprise!"

Our group leaves a handsome tip and we saunter slowly back up the hill for one final night at the Svoboda.

******

A multilayer buttercream torte decorated with crushed hazelnuts and chocolate shavings is placed in the middle of the table in a Tatar tearoom on the outskirts of Simferopol. Viktor, the driver for John and Mary, instructs the waitress to cut the cake equally into seven large pieces.

I'm taken aback by the thick layers of cream holding the cake together but am nonetheless eager to conquer my gigantic slice. The torte is masterfully prepared, delicately balancing sweet butter and sugar against the sharpness of hazelnuts and rich, bittersweet dark chocolate. Served with mint tea, the afternoon treat is the perfect conclusion to our Crimea dining experiences.

Yevgeny and Viktor open up about their personal backgrounds. Iryna translates that both have large families and are devout Muslims. They've known each other since high school. They've lived in Crimea all their lives but could not express their faith under Soviet rule. Since Ukraine gained her independence in 1991, and with the return of Tatars to Crimea, the Muslim faith is enjoying a resurgence.

On our last drive to the children's home, the car is silent. I'm deep in thought, mentally preparing to radiate serene contentment so that our son's transition to his new world is as normal a day as any. Aware of the ritual that's about to unfold, I'm battling extreme feelings of happiness and sadness, both at the same time.

As my husband and I enter the building, we note the elderly administrator is sporting her Canadian maple leaf toque and matching scarf. She grins as we pass her desk. I force myself to slow down, push my shoulders back, and take long, deep breaths. Albert, Iryna, and I march down the dark hallways toward room S-11 for the last time.

Iryna hands Erik's release papers to a physician who is waiting for us in the anteroom. The doctor reads the papers, signs them, and instructs us to remain in the antechamber. She's back momentarily with a caregiver holding Erik in her arms. The woman removes all of Erik's clothes and hands him to me, naked, his feet kicking as they dangle underneath the woman's outstretched arms.

We're well prepared for the handover, as we were told in advance that all of the clothes worn by children at Yolochka never leave the premises for good. They are needed for the kids left behind.

I hug my son close to my chest and kiss him on the cheek. My husband leans in and kisses him, too.

"Mom and dad are here to pick you up," Albert says to our son in Latvian. "The three of us are going on a trip!"

I place Erik gently down on the narrow cubbyhole shelf and dress him in warm new clothes and his snowsuit for travel. Albert ties the boot laces.

A second caregiver enters the anteroom, along with an additional physician. They say brief goodbyes to Erik. Albert and I shake hands with the staff and thank them for caring for our son. Iryna informs us it's time to go. Erik's eyes dart back and forth between my husband and I.

"Ooorh! Dhizz!" he says.

As we exit the main door for the last time, I stop, turn around, and take a final look at the place where my son has lived for more than a year.

"This is it. We'll all be together now," I quietly tell my son.

Yevgeny pops open the back door of his sedan. Erik is positioned between my husband and I. We strap him in with a seatbelt, as there is no car seat. Our boy instinctively grabs my thumb and Albert's thumb, holding on to each of us tightly with his hands. He smiles; he knows what's up.

On the drive to Simferopol airport, I feel indescribably happy and free. Tears flow, but I quickly wipe them so as not to alarm my son.

Iryna stands at the terminal entrance with our airline tickets. She hands them to Albert.

"The adult first class seats were forty dollars American each, and the child's, forty cents. That's eighty dollars and forty cents. As you are sharing the cost of my ticket with John and Mary, it is another $20 on top of that for my ticket."

"Thank you, Iryna. It's kind of you to take such good care of us," Albert gushes. He hands her some money and tells her to keep the change.

The four of us meet John, Mary, and their children in the airport departure lounge, which is nearly empty. The mood is electric. The children can't believe their eyes. Fragrant planters of flowers and lush greens are placed throughout the gleaming terminal. The kids run spontaneously among blue leather chairs, shiny garbage cans, and side tables, smiling and laughing. No one tells them to be quiet or to stop jumping or sliding under the seats. It's exhilarating to watch.

Once on the plane, the kids sip orange soda pop from straws in glass bottles while the rest of us catch our breath. I love watching my son take such an interest in the drinking straw in his hand. He twirls it around, twists it, bends it, and looks inside. The absolute best part of the day, though, is knowing there won't be anyone coming to take my son away as he disappears behind a door. I turn my head gently away from Erik and cry silently into my sweater. My love for him is overwhelming.

Goodbye, Ukraine

For our remaining days in Ukraine, Sofia has a arranged a studio apartment in Kyiv that we are renting from an elderly acquaintance of hers. The city is bitterly cold and blanketed with snow, but the fifth-floor apartment Albert, Erik, and I are enjoying is warm.

We're shown by the apartment owner, the elderly lady Sofia knows, how to convert the couch into a bed and the proper way to ignite the starter for the gas stove in the kitchen using wooden matches.

Sofia instructs us to leave our suitcases unpacked. We have an early evening appointment at the Embassy of Canada to go over some documents, followed by dinner out with our whole group. Sofia and the older lady leave us for a short time. I'm grateful for the time alone with my husband and son.

Albert flops down on the couch and taps the cover of a book he's about to start reading, *A World Lit Only by Fire: The Medieval Mind and the Renaissance*.

"I've been meaning to get to this," he tells me elatedly.

From the apartment window, I can see a large public park with tall trees and shrubs across the street below. There's an ice-covered playscape in the middle of an open area of the grounds.

While the park is inviting, it reminds me of disquieting news we've just heard: a Ukrainian investigative journalist, Georgiy Gongadze, who disappeared several months ago, was found in a forest near Kyiv, beheaded.

Gongadze was a fearless critic of Ukrainian President, Leonid Kuchma; he exposed corruption in the highest ranks of government. Rumours are circulating that the journalist was murdered on Kuchma's orders to silence him and to terrify the population.

I turn to look at my son, who is smiling at me as he drags my suitcase handle, trying to pull the heavy bag across the room. I'm shaken by the news of the journalist, but knowing we'll soon be heading home to Canada appeases me.

Erik is simply charming in his tiny blue jeans and red fleece Roots sweatshirt. I know I'll never forget this moment. From now on, our family will always be together.

At the Embassy of Canada, I'm surprised at how well our son is behaving. Everything is new to him and undoubtedly strange yet apparently much to his liking. My son sits patiently on my lap in the embassy vestibule and doesn't fuss through the hour-long wait. In our meeting with Svitlana to review and sign the papers she's prepared, Erik stares intently at the map of Canada behind her desk.

He allows Svitlana to take his hand and leans his head softly in against my chest as I read through the papers in front of me. He doesn't let out a peep. Albert places Erik on his lap in the car ride to dinner. Erik gazes out the window, watching cars zip by, and points as snow kicks up against the glass.

We meet Sofia, Iryna, and John, Mary and their children at a casual restaurant on a quiet side street in Kyiv that seems to specialize in soup. We present our Ukrainian consultants with flowers, chocolates, and perfume. Sofia and Iryna are gracious and warm in expressing their appreciation. I know these two ladies will hold a special place in my heart forever for the extraordinary task they achieved on our behalf. The gift of our son is immeasurable.

I'm more exhausted than hungry, but manage to eat half of my borscht. Erik finishes everything offered to him, including his own soup, the remainder of mine, and half of my husband's. He devours the delicious hearth-baked whole grain bread on our plates. We order fruit pastries for dessert. My son consumes all three portions and downs a tall glass of buttermilk.

I'm too enthralled with Erik to make much dinner conversation, but it's wonderful hearing from Sofia that her son is married and has a young child. Her son and family live in Kyiv so I imagine Sofia and her spouse have plenty of opportunities to visit. Iryna is thrilled to be back with her husband, too; I secretly hope her plan to become a mother will one day come true.

Albert and John amuse each other with bad jokes, and Mary and I ignore them. We exchange addresses with the American-Canadian couple, take some final photos of everyone, wish each other well, and say goodbye. Our journey together has come to its rightful conclusion.

Having received the precious gift of our children, there's nothing more to say. We've been blessed to have survived the journey so well, and I'm thankful for the company we've had along the way. Our story has a joyous ending, and an exhilarating new beginning.

The three Upeslacis return to our apartment. Albert and I are completely drained and alert at the same time. Erik is wide awake and curious. My husband gives him the stuffed teddy bear to play with. Our son hugs the bear but then quickly throws his plush plaything across the room. I decide to give my son a bath to calm him down in preparation for bed. It's nearly midnight.

What an amazing experience to finally bathe my boy in warm water! The bath gel I've brought from Canada is put to good use. Erik giggles excitedly at the eucalyptus scented bubbles floating in the tub. He splashes the water up and laughs when it falls back down onto him. I let him enjoy every second of the warm bath, thanking God for his cheerful presence. Readying Erik for bed, I dress him in a soft yellow sleeper and position him at the side of the bed by the wall beside me. Albert snuggles in on the other side of me. Within seconds, we're all asleep.

Early the next morning, I wake up to see Erik quietly sitting in bed, smiling at me. "Ooorh!" he declares.

"Ooorh," I say back to him, my voice groggy.

I sit up and lift my son towards me to hug and kiss him. I feel his soaking wet diaper against my pajama. I tap my husband's shoulder to rouse him.

"Honey, I need to step over you. Sorry. I have to change Erik's diaper."

Albert mumbles and rolls onto his other side. I carefully step across my spouse's body to get out of bed, Erik cradled up against me. It feels natural, so right for us all to be together.

I will love and cherish this boy for the rest of my life. I'm finally and officially his mother; my love for him is pure and real and unwavering.

The wall clock in the kitchen reads 6:00. The sun has not yet risen. As I'm carrying Erik into the kitchen, he points to a spoon on the kitchen counter.

"Ah! Ah!"

I search through my suitcase for a package of dry baby cereal. I boil some water, add the cereal, and watch my son consume every spoonful.

Boris, the Kyiv driver, takes us to a diner with an internet cafe so Albert and I can have breakfast and send an email home informing family of our imminent arrival. Iryna has managed to secure three tickets for a Kyiv-Toronto flight in two days' time.

The email I'm sending home to my parents is an immense pleasure to compose.

"We are arriving on flight 5873 from Frankfurt at 20:30 Toronto time on Thursday December 17. Please bring our child's car seat with you to the airport."

******

"It's a boy!" is scrawled across big blue helium balloons bobbing above the throng of people in the arrivals area at Toronto's Pearson International Airport. The balloons float towards us as we move closer to the crowd.

"Congratulations!" Laryssa Hrehoriv says, making her way to us and handing the balloons to Albert along with a bottle of champagne.

"Oh! Thank you."

"What a beautiful son you have! I'm very happy for you." Laryssa gently touches Erik's cheek.

"Yes. Thanks," I say, nearly out of breath. "I can't tell you how grateful we are for your help. It's not something I could even describe ..."

Laryssa hugs me, greets my husband, and then steps back. Directly behind her are my parents, aunt, and uncle.

After eighteen hours of travel and more than five weeks away from home, I'm overcome with emotion and can barely remain standing. I stare at each of my family members, who have waited patiently to meet our son. Tears flow.

"Here is your grandson," I say, leaning in to show my small son to my parents, my voice trembling. "This is Erik."

My family silently marvels at the beautiful little child asleep in my arms.

"He is absolutely perfect," my father says. "Dreams can come true."

Yolochka Children's Home, Simferopol, Ukraine

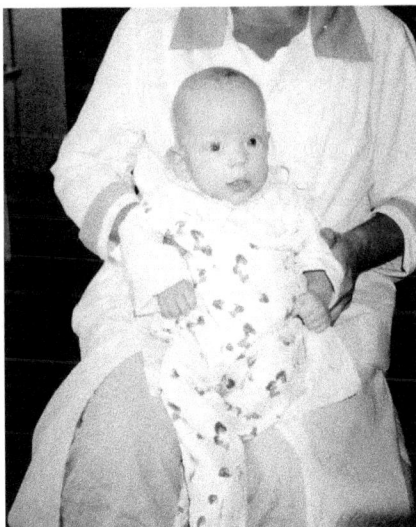

Erik upon his arrival at Yolochka Children's Home,
Simferopol, Ukraine, 1999

Albert, Erik, and Sandra at Yolochka Children's Home,
Simferopol, November 2000

Albert and Erik at Yolochka, Simferopol, November 2000

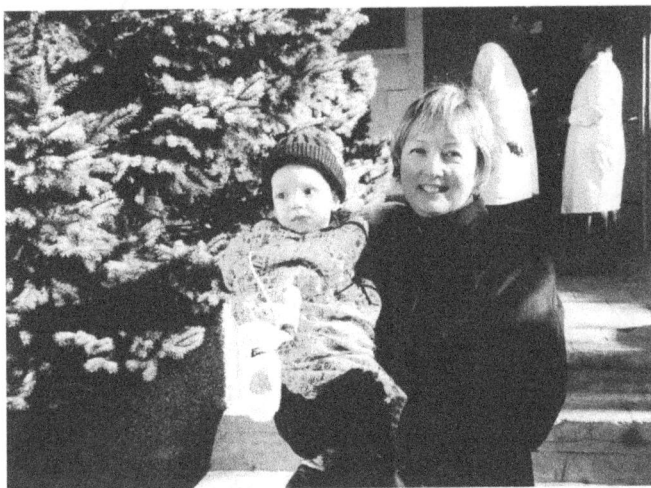

Sandra and Erik at Yolochka, Simferopol, November 2000

Erik with Albert's backpack at Yolochka Children's Home,
Simferopol, December 2000

Erik on his way to his first day of school, Junior Kindergarten,
Toronto, Canada, September 2003

Canada 2024

Time flies when you're having fun!

My beautiful son, Erik, as shy and sweet as the first day we met, is now a young man living in a small Ontario, Canada town surrounded by nature.

Raised in Toronto, Erik spent many childhood summers roaming the woods of our family cottage property and swimming in Georgian Bay. Beginning at a young age, Erik embraced outdoor pursuits, from skateboarding to BMX cycling, tobogganing, and snowboarding. A former Boy Scout, he loves to chop wood, build fires in the woods, and sleep in a tent.

Erik followed his lifelong passion for all things mechanical to forge a career. At age twenty-two, he bought his first vintage Harley-Davidson motorcycle with his own savings. After obtaining a college certificate in motorcycle and motorsports mechanics, Erik is working as a motorcycle mechanic and loves to ride his motorcycle to work, when weather permits.

Erik met his first serious girlfriend at age eighteen, the day after his beloved grandmother died. They remain inseparable.

The End

Appendix

Anderson, Jennifer. "Foreign Adoptions on the Rise." *Kyiv Post*, August 10, 2000.

Applebaum, Anne. *Iron Curtain: The Crushing of Eastern Europe, 1944-1956.* Toronto: Signal, 2012.

Applebaum, Anne. *Red Famine: Stalin's War on Ukraine.* Toronto: Signal, 2017.

Bates, Theunis. "Ukraine's Fraught Relationship with Russia: A Brief History." *The Week*, January 8, 2015.

Green, Mark A. "Crimean Tatars and Russification." *Stubborn Things: A Blog of the Wilson Centre.* September 13, 2022. https://www.wilsoncenter.org/blog-post/crimean-tatars-and-russification.

Haynes, Suyin. "How Leonard Cohen's *Hallelujah* Became an Undisputed Classic." *Time*, November 11, 2016. https://time.com/4567693/leonard-cohen-hallelujah-history/

Hopkins-Best, Mary. *Toddler Adoption: The Weaver's Craft.* Indianapolis: Perspectives Press, 1997.

Kamenev, Marina. "A leaky roof and backstage drama at Chekhov's White Dacha." *The Guardian*, November 27, 2008. https://www.theguardian.com/culture/2008/nov/17/anton-chekhov-dacha-museum-yalta

Karen, Robert. *Becoming Attached: First Relationships and How They Shape Our Capacity to Love.* New York and Oxford: Oxford University Press, 1998.

Noble, John and Ryan Ver Berkmoes. *Lonely Planet: Russia, Ukraine & Belarus*. Hawthorn: Lonely Planet, 2000.

The Parent Network for the Post-institutionalized Child. *Introductory Digest*. Adoption from Ukraine Internet Club, *W&M Digest*, May 19, 2000.

The Parent Network for the Post-institutionalized Child, *The Long-Term Effects of Institutionalization on the Behavior of Children from Eastern Europe and the Former Soviet Union*. Adoption from Ukraine Internet Club, *W&M Digest*, May 5–6, 2000.

Šnore, Edvīns, dir. *The Soviet Story*. 2008.

Statistics Canada. *Census Profile, 2016 Census*. (Catalogue no. 98-316-X2016001). November 29. 2017. Last modified October 27, 2021. https://www12.statcan.gc.ca/census-recensement/2016/dp-pd/prof/details/page.cfm?Lang=E&Geo1=PR&Code1=01&Geo2=PR&Code2=01.

Utrecht, Herr Bert, Igor Paskaloff, Vic_IV, and Sam I Am [usernames]. "Yalta." Travellerspoint. Last modified January 9, 2019. https://www.travellerspoint.com/guide/Yalta/.

"Yalta." Discover-Ukraine.info. Accessed January 25, 2024. https://discover-ukraine.info/index/crimea/yalta.

"Yalta." Wikipedia. Accessed January 25, 2024. https://en.wikipedia.org/wiki/Yalta.

Disclaimer

This is a work of creative nonfiction. All of the events in this book are true to the best of the author's memory. Some names and identifying features were changed to protect the privacy of certain parties.

The author in no way represents any public or private entity, government agency, business, consulting or professional service, or non-profit agency.

The views expressed in this book are solely those of the author.

This publication is intended to provide reliable information regarding the subject matter covered. However, it is produced with the understanding that the author and publisher are not engaged in rendering any professional advice.

Every attempt has been made to identify and credit appropriate sources of information included in this publication.

Acknowledgements

Many people had a hand in the development of this book. Thank you to Erik, for agreeing to have his early life story told. Thank you to Albert, for significant editorial support related to the sequence and substance of events in Ukraine in 2000. Thank you to those individuals in the book, whose identities are safeguarded, for reviewing the manuscript and providing constructive input. Thank you to Sonia Kondrat for invaluable editing and content expertise. Thank you to those whom read various drafts of the book and helped with fine tuning—Emily Grilo, Myra Kuksis, and Jo-Anne Ryan. Thank you to FriesenPress for expert counsel and publishing support.

9 781038 303196